TRAINING FOR WARRIORS

TRAINING FOR WARRIORS

The Ultimate Mixed Martial Arts Workout

MARTIN ROONEY

Collins

An Imprint of HarperCollinsPublishers

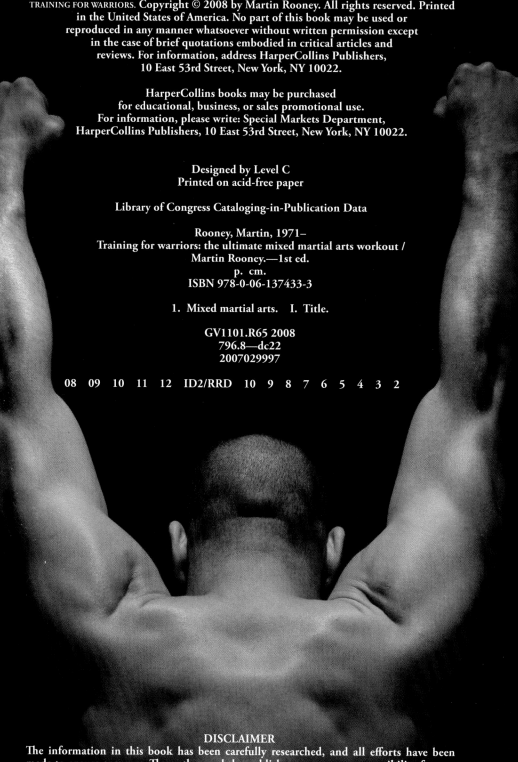

HarperCollins books may be purchased for educational, business, or sales promotional use. For information, please write: Special Markets Department, HarperCollins Publishers, 10 East 53rd Street, New York, NY 10022.

Designed by Level C
Printed on acid-free paper

Library of Congress Cataloging-in-Publication Data

Rooney, Martin, 1971–
Training for warriors: the ultimate mixed martial arts workout /
Martin Rooney.—1st ed.
p. cm.
ISBN 978-0-06-137433-3

1. Mixed martial arts. I. Title.

GV1101.R65 2008
796.8—dc22
2007029997

08 09 10 11 12 ID2/RRD 10 9 8 7 6 5 4 3 2

DISCLAIMER
The information in this book has been carefully researched, and all efforts have been made to ensure accuracy. The author and the publisher assume no responsibility for any injuries suffered or damages or losses incurred during or as a result of following the exercise program in this book. All of the procedures, poses, and postures should be carefully studied and clearly understood before attempting them at home. Always consult your physician or qualified medical professional before beginning this or any diet and exercise program.

CONTENTS

FOREWORD

Although mixed martial arts may be new to you, this sport has been part of my life for as long as I can remember. Over the last 70 years, members of my family have represented the system of martial arts that they developed in no-holds-barred events against other systems from around the world. In 1996 I left Brazil to spread my family's martial art of Brazilian Jiu Jitsu to the United States. I started my first academy in New York City, and since that time, my academy has produced champions in the Ultimate Fighting Championship (UFC) such as Matt Serra, in Pancrase such as Ricardo Almeida, and at the Abu Dhabi Combat Club (ADCC) such as Roger Gracie. During the past decade, there have been a number of students that have helped me to advance my art and one of them is Martin Rooney.

I remember early on giving Martin the nickname "the Strong One" because even though he was not very technical, his strength and speed were saving him against some of the techniques that I had developed. This fact interested me, and after getting to know Martin, we started to perform his style of physical training together starting back in 1999. This training helped me to change my physique and added strength and power to my game. After I had wins at the Pride Fighting Championships and the Abu Dhabi World Grappling Championships, my team started to notice these physical improvements that went along with my victories. At that point, many members of my family and team started training with Martin, and the Training For Warriors system was born.

In the decade since then, Martin has become like a family member of our team. He has traveled around the world to help prepare us for fights and has always evaluated his training to make sure that we were always as prepared as possible. He has always been in our team's corner and has championed the legitimacy of this sport. I understand the importance of physical training and preparation for the fighter, and I believe Martin's system produces results because he understands the demands of mixed martial arts and how to train for them. I am excited to see his work unleashed around the world and know that every fighter will benefit from the training information inside.

This book is further proof that our great sport has arrived. Now it is up to you, the reader, to take the knowledge in this book and apply it to your own training. As I always say to my students, "If you come to church, you might as well pray." You bought this book, so now you must use it to physically test yourself. I know how hard these workouts have been on me, and now it is your turn to feel the pain. Remember, my friends, you have to be the nail for a long time before you ever get to be the hammer!

Your #1 Fan,

Renzo Gracie
New York City
August 2007

Part I

MIXED MARTIAL ARTS

Martin coaching the NY Pitbulls in the ways of the warrior during a training session.

one

SO YOU WANT TO BE A WARRIOR?

Welcome to the path of the warrior. This book is your guide to growing both physically and mentally into a warrior. What is a warrior? One definition is someone who engages in or desires combat, but I believe history's greatest warriors show us that being a warrior is more about gaining control over oneself in all aspects of life.

There have been many famous cultures of the past that glorified the warrior. The Spartans, the Romans, the Persians, the Knights Templar, the Mongols, the Vikings, and the Samurai were societies that were famous for the development of their warriors. The legends of those warriors have been passed down because of the impact they made on the consciousness of the world.

The warrior tradition is still alive today. Since every generation has its warriors, we may have just lost sight of how to recognize one. A new breed of warrior has, in fact, exploded onto the landscape of the world through the vehicle of mixed martial arts. These men and women will be the role models that future generations will use as a gauge of their own warrior status. There is nothing more primal and intriguing than watching two men battle it out in a ring or cage to decide one winner and one loser. Even though this new warrior may not be battling in a life-or-death situation, the chief attributes of these modern-day warriors are the same as those of the warriors of the past.

Whether one is a fighter or just wants to train like one, anyone can develop the fitness of body and strength of character of a warrior. This book was designed to bring out the warrior in all of us. Do you think you have what it takes to be a warrior? What is the legacy you want to leave behind for future generations? You will find that the workouts in this book will test, not only your body, but also your mind. In order for you to someday be a warrior, this book is going to ask just one thing of you: all that you have. Upon completion of these warrior workouts, you will be a physically harder and mentally stronger warrior no matter what your endeavor. It is then that you will be taking your first steps down the path of the warrior.

two

THE EVOLUTION OF MIXED MARTIAL ARTS

In the last fourteen years no sport in the world has undergone more radical change than mixed martial arts (MMA). Think about it, MMA is barely over a decade old in terms of being a worldwide recognized sport. When you examine the sport from the first major event in 1993 until today, you find the metamorphosis from the original bare-knuckled, no-holds-barred, tournament-style events is due to the addition of new rules and equipment and the adoption of a single-fight-in-one-night format, weight classes, rounds, and now the team concept of the International Fight League (IFL). I would say that an even more powerful cause of the evolution of MMA is its athletes. Not to put down the fighters of the past, but today's MMA competitor not only has a radically different body, but fights extremely different. Today's MMA fighter is also better prepared technically and physically.

There have been mixed martial arts competitions dating back over one hundred years, but the Ultimate Fighting Championship (UFC) in 1993 was the first glimpse of an emerging sport. This event set in motion large-scale competitions involving multiple styles with few rules. Probably the most noticeable and unexpected result was that every fight was going to go to *the ground*. In much of

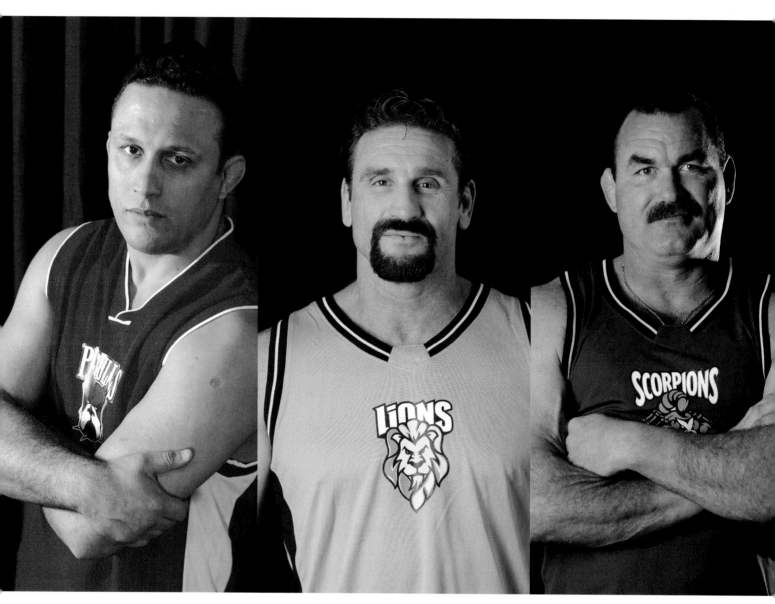

Renzo Gracie   **Ken Shamrock**   **Don Frye**

the martial arts world many people wondered which style (boxing, wrestling, karate, muay thai, judo) would prevail. Which style had the fastest, hardest punches and kicks? Which secret training methods and techniques would emerge on top? To the surprise of martial artists everywhere, all of the *striking* arts were found wanting in the face of the undersized grappler. Fighters unfamiliar with the takedown and subsequent grappling were quickly finished. Specifically, one style of grappling seemed to have an exact methodology for how to finish fights.

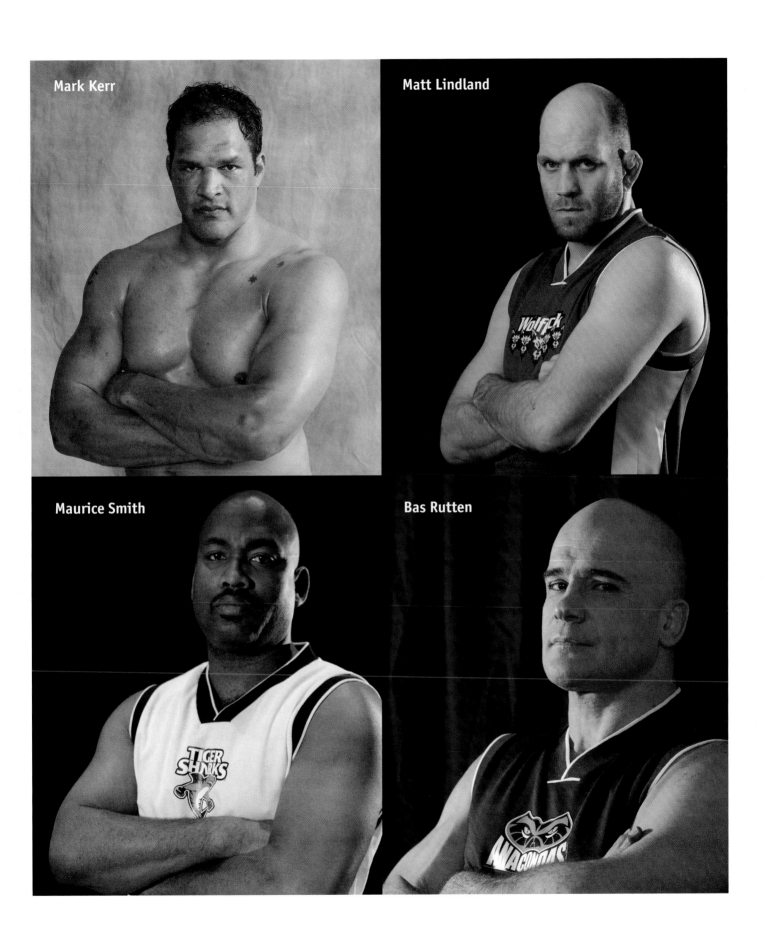

Mark Kerr

Matt Lindland

Maurice Smith

Bas Rutten

Brazilian Jiu Jitsu (BJJ) emerged as the premier style, and advanced practitioners of this art form such as Royce, Rickson, and Renzo Gracie enjoyed tremendous success and fame in the first few years. These events were tournament based, and the efficiency and methodical approach of Brazilian Jiu Jitsu reigned supreme over that of oftentimes bigger, yet less-technical and out-of-shape opponents.

After the ground game was established as a "must have" in the world of MMA, the game began to evolve. Fighters began cross-training with ground work, submissions, and submission defense. This led to the next revolution: great submission fighters could be beaten. Superior athletes such as Ken Shamrock—with some knowledge of the ground and the ability to secure a takedown, defend submissions, and deliver solid strikes from inside the opponents guard—could win the match. The next evolution in the sport was when fighters with wrestling backgrounds, such as Don Frye, started to dominate with high-level freestyle and Greco-Roman wrestling. These brutal victories that athletes such as Mark Kerr and Matt Lindland delivered were the birth of the art of "ground and pound."

These ground-and-pound fighters were as successful as the early BJJ fighters. Their great takedowns and ability to control fighters without being submitted on the ground led to many victories. But soon fighters with good strikes such as Bas Rutten and Maurice Smith began to defend takedowns and get back to their feet unscathed. Fighters now had to develop superior striking skills in addition to their wrestling and submission game. Fighters like Frank Shamrock, Pat Miletich, Carlos Newton, and Tito Ortiz started to rule the fight game. The evolution that these fighters caused takes us right to the best fighters seen today.

The most successful of today's fighters have a ground game, wrestling skills, and superior striking. Look at fighters such as Chuck Liddell, Vanderlei Silva, Randy Couture, and Fedor Emelianenko. They are some of the most dominant fighters today, and all are very strong in the technical areas just mentioned. But what if each fighter is evenly matched in skill and technique? What if each fighter has the same mind-set and the will to win? How will today's warrior continue to adapt? This is where my belief in superior fitness comes in. That is the

Frank Shamrock   Pat Miletich   Carlos Newton

next revolution in the metamorphosis of mixed martial arts: the revolution of physical preparation.

In addition to technical skill, a fighter must possess the right amount of strength, speed, power, endurance, flexibility, and mental toughness. He must also pay great attention to his nutritional and physical status to improve his performance and prevent injury. He must know how, when, and why to strategically train in certain ways at certain times. Without all of this knowledge, much of the training behind MMA is just the guesswork that has been used for centuries.

When you look at the fighters of today, you can see that this revolution has started. The days of the overweight, out-of-shape brawler are over. This is the age of the technical, conditioned, and strong SUPERFIGHTER.

I believe that a fighter's physical foundation is the cornerstone for eventual success in MMA. If a warrior is not as strong, fast, and flexible as he or she could be and has poor nutrition, that warrior will never perform to potential in the ring or on the mat. A warrior never wants to look back and know that he or she could have done more, or that the reason for a loss was not being properly physically prepared. No warrior ever wants to see an opportunity for a punch, takedown, or submission and miss it because he or she was too slow, too tired, too weak, or too inflexible to pull it off. Every warrior needs to master this knowledge about physical preparation, so that when there is the opportunity to punch, kick, knee, shoot, or submit, THEY SEIZE IT!

Mixing the martial arts has given birth to a new martial sport. There are many books on the market today on punching, kicking, grappling, and wrestling technique, but little information about how to build the physical foundation for a mixed martial artist. My intent with this book is to add into that mix the new science of building a martial warrior-athlete. *Training for Warriors* will educate the user on not only the physical-training requirements for MMA, but also how to fulfill those requirements via the exercises and methodology of the Training for Warriors program. MMA is better now than it has ever been, and will be better still with the application of the ideas found in this book. By using the science and art of physical preparation contained in this book, my goal is to help MMA to continue to evolve through the development of a BIGGER, BETTER, BADDER warrior.

three

MMA 101

Mixed martial arts is the most complex form of combat known to man. This is because MMA involves many disciplines, including boxing, wrestling, muay thai, judo, and Brazilian Jiu Jitsu. There are many different positions, strikes, takedowns, and submissions that can occur during an MMA match. The following is a comprehensive list of terms to help everyone to better understand the sport. Pay particular attention to what the athletes' bodies and muscles are doing, and try to break down how individual muscles are aiding in the fighters' ability to perform the moves.

GUILLOTINE

This submission is attained when the attacker has captured the head of the opponent under his arms with his hands interlocked and his legs interlocked around the opponent's body. This choke is powerful and can force a quick *tap out*.

SHOULDER LOCK

This is an attack to the shoulder joint in which the shoulder is hyperrotated—either internally or externally—in an attempt to force a submission.

REAR NAKED CHOKE

This submission is attained when the attacker is on the back of his opponent with his forearm squeezed against his opponent's throat. This is a very difficult choke to escape from.

TAKEDOWN

This describes any instance in which a warrior is able to get an opponent onto the ground. Takedowns can involve the entire body and are used to control the fight and gain a position on the opponent on the ground.

TRIANGLE

This is an attack in which the legs are used to trap an opponent's arm and head. The attacker then tightens his legs together and chokes the opponent in an attempt to force a submission.

CLINCH

This is a standing position in which the fighters are facing each other with the arms and upper bodies locked. This position can be used as an offensive position to deliver strikes and/or to set up the takedown. This position can also be used defensively to avoid the takedown and control the opponent.

CROSS

This is a power punch usually by the dominant hand of the striker.

LOW KICK

This is a leg strike in which the striker is attempting to either damage the leg of the opponent, keep the opponent at a distance, or set up other hand or leg strikes.

HIGH KICK

This is a leg strike in which the striker is attempting to damage the torso and head of the opponent and is ultimately looking for a *knockout*.

MOUNT

This is the second-most-dominant position in MMA. It consists of sitting on the chest of the opponent with the legs held tightly against the opponent's torso.

BACK MOUNT

This is the most-dominant position in MMA. It is attained when a warrior is seated on the back of an opponent who is lying on his stomach. The athlete on his stomach has little chance of defense.

CROSS SIDE

This position is attained when the warrior on top is lying chest to chest and perpendicular to the opponent, without the legs intertwined. This is an advantageous position for the warrior on top.

HOOK

This is a looping power punch in which the punch is thrown from the side at the opponent.

FRONT KICK

This is a straight-leg strike in which the striker is attempting to either damage the torso of the opponent or keep the opponent at a distance.

ARM BAR

This is an attack in which the arm of the opponent is hyperextended at the elbow joint in attempt to force a submission.

OPEN GUARD

This position is attained when the warrior on his back no longer has his legs intertwined, but is still attempting to control the opponent. This position is used to either create distance or return to the feet.

CLOSED GUARD

This position is attained when the warrior on top is held in between the closed and interlocked legs of the warrior on his back. This position can be advantageous to either warrior, depending on his respective skill.

JAB

This is a quick, straight punch that is used to strike the opponent. It can be used to measure the distance from the opponent, set up other strikes or takedowns, or to damage the opponent.

HALF GUARD

This position is attained when one warrior is chest to chest on top of another with one leg intertwined. This position can be advantageous to either warrior, depending on his respective skill, but usually the warrior on top has the advantage.

KNEE STRIKE

This is a powerful leg strike in which the striker is trying to damage the head or body of the opponent.

KNEE BAR

This is an attack to the knee joint in which the knee is hyperextended in an attempt to force a submission.

ANKLE LOCK

This is an attack that either manipulates the ankle joint or applies pressure to the heel or Achilles tendon in an attempt to force a submission.

TAP OUT

This is a signal of submission by the warrior. This sign for acknowledging defeat is performed by tapping the hand on either the mat, the opponent, or the warrior's own body. This is performed when the warrior is hopelessly caught in a joint lock, choke, or barrage of strikes. Upon this signal, the match has ended.

KNOCKOUT

A knockout is attained when a warrior has forced his opponent to lose consciousness via either a punch, kick, elbow, knee, or slam during the fight. Upon a knockout, the match has ended.

four

HOW TO USE THIS BOOK

In the "Warrior Anatomy" section, *Training for Warriors* devotes a chapter to each part of the body that is used in an MMA fight. The purpose of these chapters is not only to present exercises for training each body part but also to demonstrate how each region of the body is used during combat and why, therefore, each specific training is so important. Every chapter begins and ends with actual fight photos demonstrating the muscles covered. The exercises in each chapter are ordered by degree of difficulty, starting with the easiest and then working toward the most demanding. There are a range of exercises in each chapter that can be be performed using just body weight, a physioball, the body weight of a partner, and simple gym equipment.

The weight cutting and nutrition chapters provide a blueprint for properly and safely cutting weight for a competition, as well as the latest information on what to eat—including supplements—to reach maximum fitness.

At the end of the book you will find the actual warrior workouts that are followed at my gym by many successful warriors currently competing in MMA. This advanced workout is an actual 8-week plan that can be used simply to get more fit or to prepare for a fight. All of the exercises in the workouts are linked to the exercises described in detail in the "Warrior Anatomy" chapters.

Although you could complete a great workout by selecting exercises from this text without any equipment at all, I would recommend a few essential pieces of equipment that are needed to ultimately reach your potential. With a little careful shopping, you can purchase most of this equipment fairly cheaply. If you don't want to purchase any equipment, I suggest getting a gym membership at a facility that has all of the equipment listed below as well as a couple of the machines mentioned throughout the text.

EQUIPMENT FOR TODAY'S WARRIOR

barbell and weight plates

adjustable dumbbells

physioball

medicine ball

speed ladder

pulling sled

climbing rope

hammer

tire

sandbag

chin-up bar

ankle band

elastic bands

Part II

WARRIOR ANATOMY

Ken Shamrock calls on his experience to help focus the warrior mind of his fighter for the next round.

five

THE WARRIOR MIND

The mind of the warrior is just as important to work out as any muscle **of the arm, torso, or leg.** Without the cooperation of the warrior's mind with the body of the warrior, no success is possible. Although the exercises in this book will surely give any warrior more tools to be successful, without proper control over your mind, you can't reach your full potential.

When discussing the warrior mind and mind-set, it is easy to be distracted by what is going through a fighter's head during an actual MMA match. However, not only is the everyday mind of the warrior more important, but proper training of the mind in everyday situations will lead to control during an actual fight. Although you can train certain muscles of the body only every once in a while, the mind of the warrior can and must be trained consistently every day.

The mind-set of the warrior will eventually determine his destiny as a fighter, and his eventual destiny in life. To control the mind is to control one's thoughts. When this is done correctly, the warrior is able to control his actions.

Acquiring the ability to quiet the mind and stop it from running wild in emotions like fear and negativity is often one of the toughest tasks for the warrior, but through constant training and practice one can master this. The mind and the body are interrelated. Without a strong mind, a strong warrior is impossible.

Before you embark on the exercises and workouts of this book, you must first make sure that your mind is right or that you are taking the steps to improve your mind in its areas of deficiency. Below is a list of the ten characteristics of the *warrior mind-set*. You will need all of them on your warrior path. Examine each characteristic, and assess your current level in that area. If you are lacking in any of these areas, you must take action to strengthen that aspect of character as much as you would the muscles of your body.

Without the right mind-set, becoming a warrior, regardless of one's physical ability, will be impossible.

ON BEING A WARRIOR

Out of every one hundred men, ten shouldn't even be there,
Eighty are just targets,
Nine are the real fighters, and we are lucky to have them,
for they make the battle.
Ah, but the one,
One is a warrior,
And he will bring the others back.
—Heraclitus

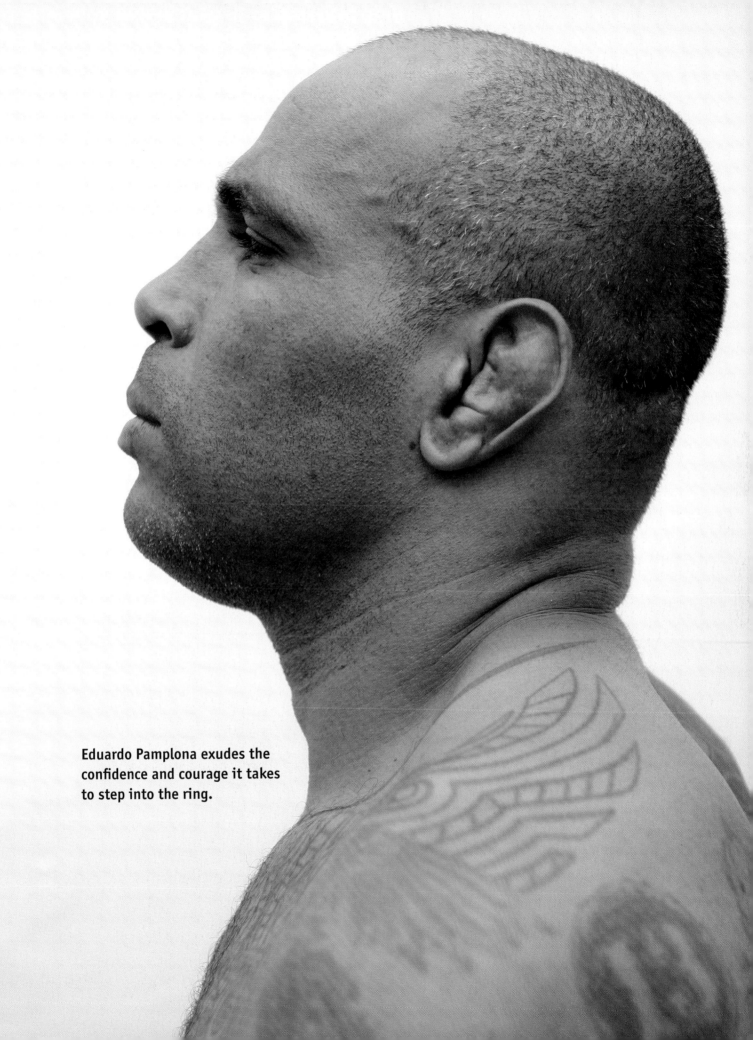

Eduardo Pamplona exudes the confidence and courage it takes to step into the ring.

1. VISION

Champions aren't made in gyms. Champions are made from something they have deep inside them—a desire, a dream, a vision. They have to have last-minute stamina, they have to be a little faster, they have to have the skill and the will. But the will must be stronger than the skill.

—Muhammad Ali

Superficial goals lead to superficial results.

—Attila the Hun

The warrior has a strong, defined vision of exactly where he wants to go. Until the vision is defined, a person has no destination. What is your vision for yourself and the future?

2. COURAGE

Whenever you meet difficult situations, dash forward bravely and joyfully.

—Tsunetomo Yamamoto, *Hagakure*

It is men who endure toil and dare danger that achieve glorious deeds, and it is a wonderful thing to live with courage and to die leaving behind an everlasting renown.

—Alexander the Great

Take arrows in your forehead, but never in your back.

—Samurai Maxim

The warrior knows that courage will be essential on his warrior quest. What he must also understand is that courage is not the absence of fear, for that is impossible. Courage is to first start and then continue moving forward toward the vision even though fear exists.

In the eye of Fabio Leopoldo you can see both the vision and desire to be champion.

3. DISCIPLINE

Victory is reserved for those who are wiling to pay its price.
—Sun Tzu

Day after day train your heart out, refining your technique: Use the one to defeat many. That is the discipline of the warrior.
—Morihei Ueshiba

Hard training, easy combat; easy training, hard combat.
—Marshal Suvorov

Without discipline, the warrior can do nothing. Not only must the warrior be prepared to do the things it takes to make his vision a reality, he must also take action. This action, taken every day, is discipline personified.

4. SELF-CONTROL

If a man does his best, what else is there?

—George S. Patton

A warrior will learn to understand that the only things he can truly control in life are his own thoughts, emotions, and actions. This control over oneself is the challenge that the warrior must face every day. The warrior must accept responsibility for his thoughts and actions if he is ever to reach true warrior status.

5. PATIENCE

It does not matter how slowly you go so long as you do not stop.

—Confucius

Every day you may make progress. Every step may be fruitful. Yet there will stretch out before you an ever-lengthening, ever-ascending, ever-improving path. You know you will never get to the end of the journey. But this, so far from discouraging, only adds to the joy and glory of the climb.

—Sir Winston Churchill

The warrior knows that any vision worth pursuing is going to take a long time to achieve. There will be many days along the warrior's path when it may not seem that progress is taking place. The warrior must *embrace* these days and push forward, knowing that staying the course is the only way to eventually reach the goal.

6. DESIRE

There is nothing impossible to him who will try.
—Alexander the Great

If a warrior does not stand for something, he will eventually fall for anything. The warrior must believe strongly in his quest and constantly keep in place reminders of why the vision was important in the first place.

7. CONFIDENCE

Go to the battlefield firmly confident of victory and you will come home with no wounds whatsoever.
—Samurai general Kenshin Uesugi

Not only must the warrior be confident in his day-to-day thoughts and actions, but the warrior must also be firmly resolved that his vision will, in fact, eventually become true. This positive mind-set is an essential tool in the warrior's arsenal.

Renzo Gracie proves that a strong mind and resilience are essential for victory.

8. RESILIENCE

Fall down seven times, get up eight.

—**Japanese proverb**

Only a man who knows what it is like to be defeated can reach down to the bottom of his soul and come up with the extra ounce of power it takes to win when the match is even.

—**Muhammad Ali**

Defeat is a state of mind. No one is ever defeated until defeat has been accepted as a reality. To me, defeat in anything is merely temporary, and its punishment is but an urge for me to greater effort to achieve my goal. Defeat simply tells me that something is wrong in my doing; it is a path leading to success and truth.

—**Bruce Lee**

The warrior that achieves the highest vision is the one who has made the most errors along the way. A warrior must recognize that success is built not on success, but on past mistakes, mishaps, and errors. The warrior embraces these errors, moves forward, and makes sure not to make the same mistakes again.

9. COMMITMENT

He who has a why to live for can bear almost any how.
—**Friedrich Nietzsche**

With it or on it.

—**Ancient Spartan motto meaning "Come back with your shield or come back on it."**

The warrior knows that the achievement of a vision can be completed only with full and focused commitment. The warrior must remove any distractions and elements from his life that will jeopardize the fulfillment of his goals. Until the warrior has fully committed, the vision is just talk about a dream.

10. RESPECT

> The Way of the Warrior is based on humanity, love, and sincerity: the heart of martial valor is true bravery, wisdom, love, and friendship.
> **—Morihei Ueshiba**

> The warrior takes his lot, whatever it may be, and accepts it in ultimate humbleness. He accepts in humbleness what he is, not as grounds for regret, but as a living challenge.
> **—Carlos Casteneda**

> The mind of the warrior, in the end, becomes nothing more than seeing things as they truly are and realizing the beauty in that simplicity.
> **—Musashi**

The warrior is not filled with hatred, nor is he a wrongdoer to others. The warrior is someone who respects all. This is the ultimate concept for the warrior who must battle an opponent. The warrior recognizes that without the opponent doing his best to complete his own vision, the warrior's experience would be cheapened. The warrior must respect his opponent, his teacher, his team, and his family. Without respect in place, the warrior wannabe is nothing more than a glorified thug.

Joe Sampieri performs the final part of his warm-up in the ring moments before the fight.

six

THE WARRIOR WARM-UP

Before a warrior can attack his workout, he must first prepare his body. The warrior warm-up makes every warrior stronger, faster, more dynamically flexible, and improves both balance and endurance. These preparatory exercises are a series of ground-based calisthenics that keep the warrior moving through the entire warm-up session.

The warrior warm-up prepares the body for the demanding activities of striking, wrestling, and grappling. This warm-up increases a fighter's core temperature, which is important for performance. With a higher temperature in the core and in the specific muscles about to be used, the warrior is ensured better performance during the workout with less chance of injury. By using the warm-up exercises through a complete range of motion, the warrior's dynamic flexibility is increased and his joints are nourished and strengthened by the compressive forces passed through them. By using the dynamic version of stretching, the neuromuscular system is prepared to perform; and by performing the exercises over and over correctly, the athlete also improves his coordination and ability to process new skills.

Remember, training is not just about getting tired. A true warrior must be more concerned with the quality of work than with its quantity and intensity. A warrior does not sacrifice technique for speed when beginning to perform this warm-up. Begin this new warm-up at a higher quality and lower intensity level. This means that even though the eventual goal is to complete the full warm-up in 20 minutes or less, the first number of times you perform this warm-up, it could take up to an hour to do it correctly. As your skill improves, you can increase the intensity to match the quality of your exercise. You *must* monitor your technique and address any errors. You must also make sure not to perform a task better on one side versus another. These unilateral mistakes must be addressed to ensure that the warrior will reach maximum athletic potential. The warrior must also remember that joint position affects specific muscle recruitment. Because of this fact, the fighter must perform the drills as they are described in this chapter in order to maximize the desired specific training effect.

Training is an all-year process. Stay consistent with the warm-up year-round so that the exercises become truly a warm-up and not a complete workout in themselves. When a warrior applies this type of consistency to his training, that will be a time of progress and, most important, the warrior will use this warm-up to better understand himself.

A NOTE ON TERMINOLOGY

For anyone familiar with basic workout techniques, but new to the terminology, there are a few words that may need to be clarified:

DORSIFLEXION: Toes pulled up toward the knee

PLANTARFLEXION: Toes pointed down away from the knee

EVERSION: Outward rotation of the sole of the foot

INVERSION: Inward rotation of the sole of the foot

SUPINE: Lying on the back

PRONE: Lying on the stomach

FLEXION: A movement that lessens the angle at a joint

ABDUCTION: Moving a body part out to the side of the body

ADDUCTION: Bringing a body part closer to the body

WARM-UP EXERCISES
Stationary Warm-up Drills

1. PRISONER SQUAT

Stand with feet wider than shoulders.

Place hands behind the head with interlocked fingers.

Sit back while bending at the knees; shins stay vertical, weight is on the heels.

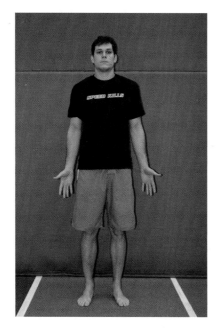 

2. JUMPING JACK

Begin with the feet together and the arms at the side.

Jump the feet apart to the side, wider than shoulder width.

Abduct arms overhead, with the elbows straight.

Return to the initial position.

Keep the knees and elbows fully extended and the ankle dorsiflexed.

3. SEAL JUMP

Begin with the feet together and the hands in front together at shoulder height.

Jump by splitting the feet apart and fully horizontally abducting the arms.

Return to the initial position.

Keep the knees and elbows fully extended and the ankles dorsiflexed.

4. HIGHLAND FLING

Begin with the feet shoulder-width apart and the arms horizontally abducted.

Jump so that the right leg crosses over the left and the arms cross midline.

Return to the initial position, and then reverse the arms and legs.

Keep the knees and elbows extended and ankles dorsiflexed.

5. POGO JUMP

Begin by standing with legs straight and arms as shown.

Stay in rigid position and jump only a few inches in the air, keeping knees extended.

Maintain dorsiflexion and quickly leave ground after landing.

Repeat jumps as fast as possible.

6. FRONT LUNGE

Begin with hands out front and left foot forward as shown.

Keep the chest vertical, and step forward on left leg.

Lower the right knee to the ground and explode back to start position.

The focus is hip-body stability; hold the position.

7. SIDE LUNGE

Begin in same position as number 6.

Step out to the side, loading that leg and keeping the feet forward.

Align the nose, knee, and toe.

Press back to original position.

8. WIDE OUT

Begin in a squat position with the knees together.

While in the squat position, jump and spread the legs past shoulder width.

The feet stay pointed forward, and the head should not change height.

Return to the initial position, and repeat.

9. GATE SWING

Begin in a squat position with the knees together and hands above the knees as shown.

While in the squat, jump and spread the legs, feet and knees pointing out.

The focus is the stretch across the groin muscles; head stays level.

Return to the original position.

Movement Warm-up Drills

10. FORWARD SKIP

Start with the left foot forward and the right
foot back, and the right arm forward and the
left arm back.

Begin the skipping action by driving the right
leg forward while driving off the left leg,
which is pushing in the down and backward
direction.

The force is violently placed into the ground on
each skip.

Maintain good, erect posture, and focus on
keeping the toes pulled up.

Make sure the arms and legs are synchronized
on every skip.

11. SIDE SHUFFLE

Begin by standing sideways to the direction you want to go, as shown.

Start to move sideways, making sure not to cross the feet.

Stay on the balls of the feet, and make sure to stay at the same height.

12. HIGH-KNEE CARIOCA

Begin by standing sideways to the direction you want to go, straight up and tall.

Drive the left knee up so that it steps over and crosses the opposite knee.

Place the left foot on the floor.

Step out with the right foot.

Step the left foot behind the right, and repeat the pattern.

13. WALKING HIGH KICK

Begin walking forward.

Every third step, kick the foot in the air as high as possible with the knee straight.

Touch the toes with the opposite hand.

Take 3 more steps and repeat on other side.

14. FRONT-LUNGE WALK

Start with the left foot forward and the right foot back, and the right arm forward and the
 left arm back.

Step out with the right foot and switch the arm position.

Land on the right foot and sink the body down over it.

Then drive up and pull left leg through and switch arms.

15. SIDE-LUNGE WALK

Start in the athletic position, keeping the hips low.

Drive the right foot and hand out to the side and cover the face with the left hand.

Keep the heel turned outward on the right foot.

Move the body back over the right foot and repeat.

Stay at the same height the entire distance.

Muscle Activation Exercises

16. DOUBLE-LEG BRIDGE

Begin on the back, with the knees bent and the feet flat on the floor.

Press the heels into the ground and lift the hips as high as possible.

Lower under control and repeat.

17. SINGLE-LEG BRIDGE

Begin on the back, with the knees bent and one foot flat on the floor.

The other knee is held at 90 degrees with the toes pulled up toward the knees.

Press the heel into the ground and lift the hips as high as possible.

Lower under control and repeat.

18. STRAIGHT-LEG RAISE

Begin by lying on the back, with the head on the floor, legs straight, and toes pulled up.

Kick foot up toward ceiling, and return toward the floor.

Do not touch the leg back to the floor, maintain ankle position.

19. OUTSIDE-LEG RAISE

Begin by lying on one side, with the shoulders, hip, and ankle forming a straight line.

Keep toes pulled up and point top heel to the ceiling.

Lift the leg to the side through the full range of motion, and lower under control.

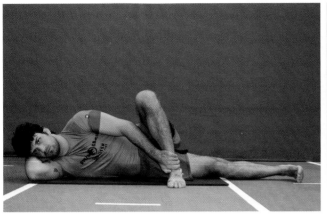 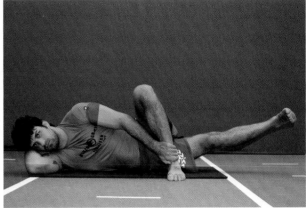

20. INSIDE-LEG RAISE

Begin by lying on one side, top leg crossing over bottom, with the top leg's foot flat on
   the floor.

Bottom leg is kept straight, with the ankle in dorsiflexion.

The bottom leg is lifted maximally, with no rotation at the hip.

21. INSIDE SWEEP

Begin by lying on one side, with the top foot flat on the floor behind the knee of the
   straight bottom leg.

Lift the bottom leg as high as possible while keeping the foot parallel to the floor.

Lower under control, and repeat.

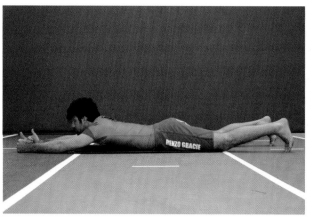 

22. ALTERNATING ARM/LEG RAISE

Begin by lying prone on a mat, with the arms extended forward and the legs straight.

The thumbs can be pointed to the sky, and the ankles must be kept dorsiflexed.

Lift the left arm and right leg simultaneously, then lower them, keeping both straight.

Then do the same with the opposite limbs; make sure dorsiflexion is kept.

23. SUPERMAN

Begin by lying prone on a mat, with the arms extended forward and the legs straight.

The thumbs are pointed to the sky, and ankles are kept dorsiflexed.

Lift both arms and legs at the same time, keeping the limbs straight.

Try not to let the thighs or arms touch the ground between reps.

24. FIRE HYDRANT

Begin by kneeling with hands on the floor and both ankles dorsiflexed.

Keep the hands under the shoulders and the knees under the hips.

The shoulders and hips are kept square and parallel to the ground.

Keep the knee bent so the calf touches the hamstring.

Bring the knee up and point the thigh backward at a 45-degree angle.

25. FIRE HYDRANT FORWARD CIRCLE

Begin in the hydrant position explained in number 24.

Rotate the thigh so the knee scribes a large circle forward.

Maintain dorsiflexion, and keep the back from rotating and the
   arms straight.

Shoulders and hips are kept square and parallel to the ground.

26. FIRE HYDRANT BACKWARD CIRCLE

Begin in the hydrant position explained in number 24.

Rotate the thigh so the knee scribes a large circle backward.

Maintain dorsiflexion, and keep the back from rotating and the
  arms straight.

Shoulders and hips are kept square and parallel to the ground.

27. FIRE HYDRANT STRAIGHT SIDE-LEG RAISE

Begin in the hydrant position explained in number 24.

Straighten and abduct one leg perpendicular to the line of the body.

Lift the straight leg to the maximum abduction, and return it to the floor but do not
  rest it there.

Maintain dorsiflexion, and keep shoulders and hips square.

28. BACK-LEG RAISE

Begin in the hydrant position explained in number 24.

Straighten and extend one leg straight back, in line with the body.

Keeping dorsiflexion, maximally extend the leg at the hip above shoulder.

Shoulders and hips are kept square and parallel to the ground.

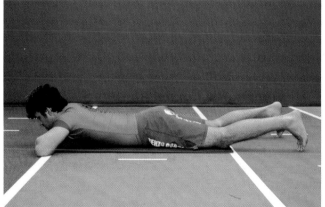

29. PRONE KNEE RAISE

Begin by lying on the stomach, with the hands under the chin.

Drive the knee up toward the elbow on the same side.

Do not touch the ground with the leg, and return to the original position.

30. SCORPION

Begin in the prone position, with the arms out to the side, palms down.

Reach back with folded left leg to try to touch heel to right hand.

Maintain the dorsiflexion during the exercise.

After touching the hand, rhythmically roll and switch sides.

31. IRON CROSS

Begin in the supine position, with arms out to the sides.

Sweep the straight left leg across the body to the opposite hand.

Turn the head in the opposite direction of the leg, and keep toes up.

Keep the stationary leg on the midline and stabilize leg during movement.

32. ROLLOVERS TO INSIDE HURDLER SEAT

Begin seated on the ground, with the legs extended to the sides of the body and toes up.

Roll back and touch the toes to the floor, and then roll back to sitting position.

Stretch forward in the hurdler seat position shown and roll backward again.

Reverse legs in the hurdler seat position upon return.

Upper-Body Warm-up

1. TIGER CRAWL

Begin on the hands and feet in the
   push-up position, as shown.
Move the opposite arm and leg
   forward while keeping the hips low.
Bring the knee up to the elbow and
   then repeat on the other side.

2. GORILLA CRAWL

Begin on the knuckles and the feet with the hips in the air, as shown.

Swing the hips out to the side of the hand that is farthest from the body.

Then switch the hands and swing the hips to the other side.

Move forward, alternating this pattern.

3. FROG HOP

Begin in the frog position with the hips low and chest up, as shown.

Lean forward in preparation to hop forward onto the hands.

Jump out forward and place only the hands on the ground.

Bring the feet forward and outside the hands to the original frog position.

4. CRAB WALK

Begin seated on the buttocks with only the hands and feet touching the ground, as shown.

Move the same side's foot and hand backward simultaneously.

Then move the other side's foot and hand backward.

5. SPIDER CRAWL

Begin in the low tiger position, as shown.

As you crawl forward with opposite hands and feet, lower the ear and body to the floor
between each step.

Push the body back up to the tiger position, and take another step.

6. SIDE CRAWL

Begin in the push-up position with the feet wide apart, as shown.

Cross the right arm over the left and bring the feet together.

Bring the left arm back out to the left and feet back apart to achieve the original position.

7. HIP ESCAPE

Begin in the push-up position, as shown.

Keep the left hand and right foot on the ground as you switch the left foot under the body and then up to the right, as shown.

Return to the push-up position, and repeat on the opposite side.

Upper-Body Warm-up: The Medicine Ball

This circuit is to be repeated 3 times completely. Use anything from a 1- to an 8-pound ball. A 6-pound ball is an excellent choice for most athletes. The pace should be kept rapid. The athletes should stand about 3–4 yards apart and throw to one another, or one athlete can use a wall, as shown.

8. STRAIGHT STANDING SIDE PASS

Stand facing the wall with the ball held behind the hip.

Twist and throw the ball into the wall as if throwing a bucket of water.

As the ball returns off the wall, catch the ball, twist maximally, and return the ball to the
wall as if throwing a bucket of water.

9. STANDING BACKWARD WRAPAROUND THROW

Stand facing away from the wall with the ball held out in front.

Twist the upper body and look back at the wall while throwing the ball to the wall.

Catch the ball on the rebound, and return to original position.

10. STANDING CHEST PASS

Hold the ball at chest level facing the wall.

Press the ball forward into the wall and keep the elbows extended waiting to receive the ball on the rebound.

Absorb the returning ball by bending the elbows, and then repeat throw.

11. OVERHEAD KNEELING PASS

Hold the ball overhead while facing the wall.

Throw the ball forward into the wall using a soccer-throw motion.

Keep the hands and arms overhead to receive the ball on the rebound.

Absorb the ball by bending at the elbows and allowing a great stretch of the triceps.

12. STRAIGHT KNEELING SIDE PASS

Kneel facing the wall with the ball held behind the hip.

Twist and throw the ball into the wall as if throwing a bucket of water.

When the ball returns off the wall, catch it, twist maximally, and return the ball to the wall
   as if throwing a bucket of water.

13. PERPENDICULAR KNEELING SIDE PASS

Kneel facing perpendicular to the wall with the ball held behind the hip.

Twist and throw the ball into the wall as if throwing a bucket of water.

When the ball returns off the wall, catch it, twist maximally, and return the ball to the wall
   as if throwing a bucket of water.

14. ONE-ARM ROTATOR CUFF DRIBBLE

Begin with chest close to the wall and hold the ball in one hand overhead.

Dribble the ball against the wall as quickly as possible.

Perform exercise on both sides.

15. KNEELING BACKWARD WRAPAROUND THROW

Face away from the wall with the arms extended in front holding the ball.
Twist the upper body, look back at the wall, and throw the ball to the wall.
Catch the ball on the rebound, and return to the original position.

John Marsh controls the body of Chad Griggs by first controlling the head and neck.

seven

WARRIOR NECK TRAINING

Every warrior should know that if you can control the head, you can **control the body.** Since the neck is the sole connection between the head and the body, every warrior should easily see the importance of properly training this area. Yet though the neck is one of the most important body parts of the warrior, this region is often the most underworked area of the mixed martial artist's body. The ultimate goal is to have a muscular neck so thick and strong that no person can tell where the ears end and the shoulders begin.

For the mixed martial artist, the neck is critical for success in the ring for a number of reasons. The neck is often used in maintaining posture in the clinch while standing, as leverage during takedowns and takedown defense, and to support the weight and balance of the body during ground work. Not only will weakness in the neck potentially lead to poor performance, but injury is sure to happen eventually. Injury prevention is paramount for the neck, since this area of the body is one of the most commonly attacked in submission attempts— such as the rear naked choke, guillotine, and various neck cranks—and is essential in the transfer of forces during vicious strikes to the head. When there is injury to the neck, training may be limited, so the exercises contained in this chapter are critical.

The ultimate goal of the neck training in this book is to develop a neck that is not only strong, but durable. The exercises in this chapter will create this type of neck, but only through smart training. Since many muscles of the neck are small and often underworked, begin training this area conservatively. Start with one session of neck training per week, see how you recover, and eventually move up to a maximum of two specific training sessions per week. The exercises listed below are in order of intensity, so begin with the easiest first. Do not attempt all of the exercises during one session.

By following the workouts outlined at the end of this book, you will gradually work up, over a number of weeks, to the more difficult exercises. Any exercise that causes pain should be removed from your training. When you are training your neck, it is very important to maintain proper technique. Remember that we are training the neck to prevent future injuries, not cause them. Use slow, controlled tempos, and don't jerk or bounce in any of the positions. Do not forget, before you begin any training session, make sure you properly warm up first with the warrior warm-up and then the neck warm-up exercises described in this chapter. The warrior warm-up will increase your heart rate and body temperature, and then you can work specifically on warming up the neck. Finally, you must make sure that you keep your jaw closed and your tongue pressed against the roof of your mouth during training of the neck. Since changes in head position affect the articulation of the jaw and the skull, it is important to keep this joint locked by biting down during the exercises. Not only will this strengthen the jaw, it will teach good habits for the ring as well.

NECK EXERCISES
Neck Warm-up

A good neck warm-up would be to flex your neck and head forward and extend them backward, and turn your head from left to right and then right to left, for 20 reps of each movement.

1. LYING FLEXION AND EXTENSION

Lie on your back on a bench, with the head hanging over the edge.

Hang the head backward as far as possible and slowly bring the chin as close to the chest as possible.

Repeat for 20 repetitions.

NECK-TRAINING EXERCISES

Neck Isometric Resistance

One basic method for training the neck is manual isometric resistance. This is effective, takes little time, and can be done alone using the hands or a physioball.

2. MANUAL RESISTANCE

Place the heel of your hand(s) on the side of your head or on your forehead.

Apply pressure with your hand(s), and resist with your neck without allowing the head to move.

Begin with easy pressure and work up to pressing as hard as you can, as long as you are able to keep your neck still against the resistance.

Physioball Neck Leans

Instead of using the hands, you can also use a stability ball to make the exercise more comfortable. The three stability ball exercises pictured are as follows:

3. FORWARD BALL LEAN

Place the ball against the wall, and then place the forehead against the ball to hold it in place.

Then lean the body weight forward to increase the resistance.

Hold for 10 breaths.

4. BACK BALL LEAN

Place the ball against the wall, and then place the back of the head against the ball to hold it in place.

Bend the legs and lean back into the ball to increase the resistance.

Hold for 10 breaths.

5. SIDE BALL LEAN

Place the ball against the wall, and then place the side of the head against the ball to hold it in place.

Take the foot closest to the wall off the ground and lean in to increase the resistance.

Hold for 10 breaths, and repeat on each side.

6. PRONE COBRA EXTENSION

Lie on the stomach, with arms at a 45-degree angle to the body and the palms down.

Lift chest and arms off the floor.

Pinch the shoulder blades back and lift hands as high as possible.

Rotate thumbs up to the sky.

Hold the position for 5 seconds.

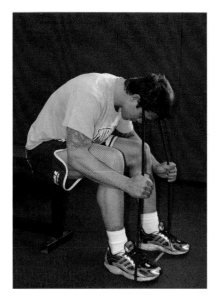  

7. BAND NECK TRAINING

Sit on a bench with one end of the band beneath the feet.

Wrap the other end of the band behind the head, and bend completely forward.

Sit up straight and pull back the head while extending the arms to create more tension.

Hold the position for 5 seconds, and then slowly lower the head.

8. DUMBBELL SHRUG

Hold the dumbbells in each hand, with the elbows straight and the palms facing backward.

Bring the shoulders as close to the ears as possible, and then slowly lower them back to
   their original position.

9. INCLINE DUMBBELL CLEAN

Begin this exercise with the chest and stomach leaning against an incline bench and
  holding the dumbbells with the palms facing backward.

Shrug the upper back to squeeze the shoulder blades together, and then externally rotate at
  the shoulder, bringing the arms up, so the palms finish the exercise facing the floor.

Return to the original position.

10. BACK NECK BRIDGE (WRESTLER'S BRIDGE)

Begin on the back, with the knees bent and the palms flat on the stomach as shown.

Lift the body on the hands and feet and place the weight of the body on the top of
  the head.

Hold this position for 20 seconds.

11. FRONT NECK BRIDGE

Begin by lying on the stomach.

Place the hands behind the back and lift the hips into the air as high as possible while
placing the weight of the body on the forehead.

Hold this position for 20 seconds.

12. PARTNER SIT-UPS AND NECK EXTENSION

Partner #1 begins on the floor in the hands-and-knees position, as shown.

Partner #2 sits high on warrior #1's back while placing reverse hooks in on #1's legs.

Partner #2 leans all the way back while #1 lowers his head and maintains balance by
locking his body in place.

To complete the movement, #2 sits up and #1 assists by extending his neck.

13. BRIDGE BENCH PRESS

After the initial Back Neck Bridge is improved upon, a warrior can also use a weighted bar to perform sets of bench presses from this position as well.

Begin with weight on the chest in the Back Neck Bridge position.
Press the weight toward the ceiling and then return to the original position.

14. BACK BRIDGE PULLOVER

Begin in the Back Neck Bridge position, and grab a bar of weight lying behind the head.
Pull the weight overhead and hold the weight up over the body for 3–5 seconds before
    lowering the weight again.

15. BACK BRIDGE PARTNER PRESS

Begin in the Back Neck Bridge position, chest to chest with your partner with your hands
    placed on the partner's chest.

Press the partner upward by extending at the elbows.

Lower under control to original position.

16. PUSH-UP NECK PARTNER PRESS

Partner #1 begins in the push-up position.

Partner #2 places both hands on the back of #1's head.

Partner #2 lowers his chest to #1's head and presses back to original position.

17. PUSH-UP NECK-AND-SHOULDER PARTNER PRESS

Partner #1 begins in the push-up position.

Partner #2 places one hand on the back of #1's neck and other on his shoulder.

Partner #2 lowers his chest to #1's head and presses back to original position.

18. KNEE-ON-CHEST BENT-OVER ROW

I like this exercise to be done using a decline bench to simulate the "knee on chest" position. This allows the athlete to combine a pulling motion with the driving downward motion of the knee and hips. This combination will help to pin any opponent to the mat.

Start with the knee low on the decline and the supporting hand higher up.

Retract the shoulder blades, and then bring the weight to the chest by bringing the elbow back. Rotation of the spine at the end of the movement is optional.

Lower under control to original position.

Matt Lindland attacking the neck of Jeremy Horn from open guard.

Andre Gusmao uses his head and neck to assist in the neck attack on Wojtek Kaszowski.

Niko Vitale shows off some powerful chest and shoulder muscles against Jeremy Horn.

eight

WARRIOR CHEST AND SHOULDER TRAINING

Not only do huge shoulder and chest muscles make a warrior look more imposing, but these muscles, when properly trained, can also make him more dangerous. Without a strong set of deltoid and pectoral muscles, the warrior surely has less chance of victory and a greater chance of injury. These powerful muscles are used in almost every upper-body motion in MMA and protect the most unstable and often-attacked shoulder joint. Offensively, these muscles are essential in throwing powerful punches in stand-up, crushing an opponent in the clinch, and during takedowns and submission attempts. Defensively, these muscles are used to keep the hands up during stand-up, to pummel in and out of the clinch, and to fight off takedown attempts on the feet and submission attempts on the ground. Understanding this, the warrior must develop a set of cannonballs for shoulders that will protect the shoulder joint and demolish the opponent.

The warrior needs to understand that this area of the body is not worked best with a single pushing exercise like the bench press. Even though forms of this exercise are demonstrated in this chapter, there are many others exercises that move in different planes of motion to replicate the demands of an MMA match. Beneath the large shoulder muscles lie the four muscles called the rotator cuff. These muscles are used to decelerate the arm when punching and to rotate the arm during clinches, ground work, and submission attempts. Since these muscles are small and commonly undertrained, warriors often injure them. Many of the exercises contained in this chapter will be excellent preventative exercises to keep those muscles strong.

Since the shoulder joint is the most mobile joint of the body, there are many possible positions that the shoulder joint can attain during an MMA match. The exercises in this chapter force the warrior to make sure that the shoulder is being trained at many angles and in many directions to help stabilize this mobile and often unstable joint. Injury to this area can be devastating and career ending. These exercises will ensure that the only career that is in jeopardy is that of your opponent.

CHEST AND SHOULDER EXERCISES

1. JUDO PUSH-UP

Begin in the push-up position, with the hips as high in the air as possible.

Bring the chest down to the ground, and then push the hips through and raise the head.

Return the hips to the highest position.

2. HANDSTAND SHOULDER PRESS

Begin in the handstand position, with the feet lightly contacting the wall.

Lower the body down using the arms, and then return to the original position.

3. PARTNER WHEELBARROW DRILL

Begin in the push-up position, with the standing partner holding your legs.

Use an arm-over-arm motion to crawl across the floor.

Keep the back flat and cover the required distance.

 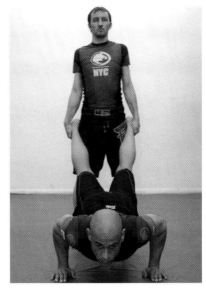 

4. PARTNER WHEELBARROW CLAP DRILL

Begin in the push-up position with the standing partner holding your legs.

With both hands at the same time, use a hopping motion to cover the distance.

Keep the back flat and attempt to clap the hands on each hop forward.

5. PARTNER PUSH-UP DRILL

Begin by lying on your back, with the partner across your chest with the hands interlocked.

Press the bent-armed partner upward and lock your elbows.

The partner then extends his arms.

Then lower the partner back to the original position.

6. MED-BALL ONE-HAND PUSH-UP

Begin in the push-up position, with the feet shoulder-width apart and one hand on the
  medicine ball.

Lower the chest to the med ball while keeping the back flat.

Press up with the arms, and then return to the original position.

7. MED-BALL TWO-HAND PUSH-UP

Begin in the push-up position, with the feet shoulder-width apart and both hands placed on
  the medicine ball.

Lower the chest to the med ball while keeping the back flat.

Press up with the arms, and then return to the original position.

8A. PHYSIOBALL PUSH-UP, HANDS ON BALL

Begin in the push-up position, with the hands on the physioball, as shown.

Lower the chest to the ball under control while keeping the back flat.

Press up with the arms, and then return to the original position.

8B. MAKE IT HARDER.

9A. PHYSIOBALL PUSH-UP, HANDS ON GROUND

Begin in the push-up position, with the hands on the floor and the toes on the physioball, as shown.

Lower the chest to the ground under control while keeping the back flat.

Press up with the arms, and then return to the original position.

9B. MAKE IT HARDER.

10A. PHYSIOBALL PIKE PRESS

Begin with the toes on the ball and the hands on the floor in the pike position, as shown.

Maintain the hips over the shoulders, and lower the head toward the ground.

Press the head back up to the original position.

10B. MAKE IT HARDER.

11. PLYOMETRIC PUSH-UP

Begin in the low push-up position up on two 6-inch boxes, as shown.

Push up explosively so that the hands leave the boxes and land on the ground.

Lower down to the ground and explode up again back on to the boxes.

12. CLOSE-GRIP BENCH PRESS

Begin by lying on the bench, with the hands in a close grip, as shown.

Lower the weight to the chest while keeping the elbows close to the body.

Press the weight back up to the original position by extending the elbows.

13. DECLINE DUMBBELL FLY

Begin by lying on the back, with the dumbbells held up in the outstretched arms overhead, as shown.

Lower the dumbbells out to the sides until a full stretch is felt.

Then return to the original position with the dumbbells held overhead.

14. WEIGHTED DIP

Begin in the high-dip position, with the elbows extended and the weight hanging from the waist, as shown.

Lower the chest under control until the elbows are at 90 degrees.

Hold this position for a 3 count, and then press up by extending the elbows to the original position.

15. DROP TRAINING FROM ROW

Begin in the high-row position, with the dumbbell held at the chest, as shown.

Drop the dumbbell and then quickly chase it with the hand to regrasp it.

Once the dumbbell is caught, return it to the original position and repeat.

This should be performed as quickly as possible.

16. DROP TRAINING TO FRONT

Begin by standing while holding the dumbbell, with the arm held out in front of the body,
    as shown.

Drop the dumbbell and then quickly regrasp.

Once the dumbbell is caught, return it to the original position and repeat.

This should be performed as quickly as possible.

17. DROP TRAINING TO SIDE

Begin by standing while holding the dumbbell, with the arm held out to the side of the body, as shown.

Drop the dumbbell and then quickly regrasp.

Once the dumbbell is caught, return it to the original position and repeat.

This should be performed as quickly as possible.

18. FLOOR PRESS

Begin by lying on the back, with the dumbbells in hand and elbows on the floor, as shown.

Press the dumbbells upward by extending at the elbows as fast as possible.

Lower under control.

19. LEANING SHOULDER FLY

Begin by hanging out to the side from a column with the foot used as a fulcrum, as shown.

From the leaning position, raise the dumbbell out to the side as high as possible.

Lower the weight under control.

20. CHAIN SHOULDER CLEAN

Begin with the chains in the hands held down at the sides with palms facing backward, as shown.

Shrug the shoulders and bring the hands up as the elbows bend to 90 degrees.

Externally rotate at the shoulders and finish in the top position, as shown.

21. CHAIN SHOULDER FLY

Begin with the chains in the hands held down at the sides with the palms facing the body, as shown.

Shrug the shoulders and bring the hands out to the sides of the body.

Raise the arms perpendicular with the torso and lower under control.

22. PLATE HIGH PULL

Hold the plate from the top and lowered in front of the chest, as shown.

Pull the plate up to chin height by raising the elbows higher than the hands.

Lower under control.

23. FRONT PLATE RAISE

Hold the plate from the sides and lowered in front of the body, as shown.

Raise the plate overhead with the arms extended at the elbow.

Lower under control.

24. PLATE TRUCK DRIVER

Hold the plate from the sides in front of the body with the elbows extended, as shown.

Twist the plate to one side so that one hand is on top and the other on the bottom of the plate.

Return to the original position, and then twist the plate in the opposite direction.

25. PLATE TRICEPS PRESS

Hold the plate from the sides and overhead, as shown.

Lower the plate behind the head, keeping the elbows high.

Raise the plate to the start position by extending the elbows.

26. AROUND-THE-HEAD PLATE DRILL

Hold the plate from the sides with the elbows bent, as shown.

Bring the plate up over a shoulder and behind the head, keeping the plate close to the body.

Return the plate back over the opposite shoulder to the original position.

27. OVERHEAD PRESS

Stand with the bar at shoulder height, as shown.

Press the weight overhead by extending the elbows.

Lower under control, and return to the original position.

TOP: Vladimir Matyushenko uses his chest and shoulder muscles to rain down punches on his mounted opponent.

BOTTOM: Jay Heiron's chest and shoulders explode into helping him shut down his opponent's shot.

Brent Beauparlant uses the strength of his grip and arms to attack the arm and shoulder of his opponent.

nine

WARRIOR ARM AND HAND TRAINING

Without a powerful set of arms and hands, the warrior is powerless against his opponent. There is nothing more impressive than a chiseled set of arms on a warrior. Even though a warrior should know that big pipes are not one of the purposes behind *Training for Warriors,* he or she should be happy to know that this will surely be a by-product of following the training program in this book.

In addition to being one of the first lines of defense, the arms and hands are also the offensive extensions of the power transferred up through the feet, legs, core, and shoulders. When this energy is transmitted properly through a stable and strong warrior, the power output of the grip and strikes from the arms and hands is nothing short of explosive. Along with powerful strikes, the arms and hands are obviously also instrumental in clinch work, wrist control, takedowns, and all submission attempts. This region of the body is also critical defensively for shielding the body and head from foot and hand strikes and for submission escapes. Without strong arms and a strong grip, it is as if the warrior has chosen to bring a knife to a gunfight.

While this chapter focuses on arms and grip, many of the exercises contained in other chapters also work this region. For instance, chin-ups and pull-ups are great exercises to train both the muscles of the arms and the grip. The exercises in this chapter are specialized exercises that were specifically designed to develop a meathook arm complemented by a bone-crushing grip. Since these are accessory exercises that are also demanding, they don't need to be performed as often as other exercises contained in this book. By following the warrior workouts at the end of the book, the warrior will see how and when to implement these exercises into his or her training.

ARM AND HAND EXERCISES

1. PLATE FINGERTIP PICK-UP

Place the fingers around the center of an Olympic plate, as shown.

Pinch down with the fingers and lift the plate from the support; hold for the required time.

Lower the plate under control.

2. PLATE PINCH DRILL

Pinch two plates of the same size and weight together.

Pinch hard and lift the plates from the support; hold for the required time.

Lower the plates under control.

3. FARMER'S WALK

This is an old-time strongman lift that we added to our program. Not only is this great for the grip, it is also a total-body strength and endurance exercise as well. You can use heavy dumbbells if you don't have the farmer's walk bars.

Pick up the dumbbells and either walk a prescribed distance for sets or see who can walk the farthest.

Release the weight at the end of the set.

4. TIRE FLIP

Begin in the kneeling position at the tire, with the hands placed outside the knees and
  gripping the tire.

Pop the feet up onto the ground without raising the hips too much.

Drive the feet into the ground, and lift the tire by standing up.

Press the tire over forcefully with the arms, and repeat for required distance.

5. ARM-OVER-ARM ROPE PULL

The rope pull is one of the most powerful and combat-specific exercises I know of. This is an incredible exercise for developing the grip, forearms, and back musculature as well as the coordination of those pulling muscles with the legs. The goal is to get as thick a rope as possible and drag anything heavy you can tie to it. Once the object is next to you, walk the rope straight out and begin again. Start gradually; your forearms will be screaming.

Begin at the far end of the rope, with the rope in both hands, as shown.
Pull each hand as far back as possible, and replace each hand farther down the rope as the sled/object gets closer.
Pull the sled to you; then walk the rope back out and repeat.

6. SANDBAG LIFT AND CARRY

A sandbag is an easy tool to make and a great tool to challenge the grip and the rest of the body. All you need is a big canvas duffel bag or two, some sand, and some duct tape, and you are ready to rock. I fill one duffel bag with a certain amount of sand, tape the bag shut, and then place that bag inside another bag and tape that one shut. This way, there is no mess and you have a great training tool. We use a 120-pound bag for bag lifts.

Squat down in front of a sandbag that is on a low box; then place your arms around the bag and lift, using a strong grip and flat back.

Stand, rotate, and then walk with the bag the required distance.

Finish by placing the sandbag on the box.

7. SANDBAG PICK-UP

Stand in front of a high box with the sandbag at the feet, as shown.

Squat down and grip the bag while keeping the back flat.

Lift the bag up onto the high box and release.

Pull the bag back to the floor and repeat.

8. FAT-BAR HOLD

A fat bar is used to challenge the grip. If you don't have a fat bar, you can place tape or clothes around the bar to make it thicker. In the gym, each athlete lifts a certain amount of weight (we usually use 225–275) and we see who can hold it the longest. This is a killer on the forearms.

Begin in the standing position, with the fat bar held in the hands, as shown.
Hold the fat bar for the prescribed time, and then release the bar.

9. BAND CURL

Begin by standing with the feet inside the band and the arms extended at the elbow, as shown.
Curl the hands to the chin while keeping the back flat and shoulders pulled back.
Lower under control.

10. BAND PUSHDOWN

Begin by standing with the head in the middle of the band and the arms bent at 90 degrees, as shown.

Press the hands down to the hips by extending at the elbows.

Raise the hands under control.

11. GI ROW

This exercise is performed by looping the gi through the holes on a rowing handle that hooks to a cable. There are three different grips that can be used, as shown: the pistol grip, the overhand grip, and the collar grip.

Begin by grabbing the gi with the chosen grip.

Keep the back flat and row the gi to the chest as high as possible.

Lower under control.

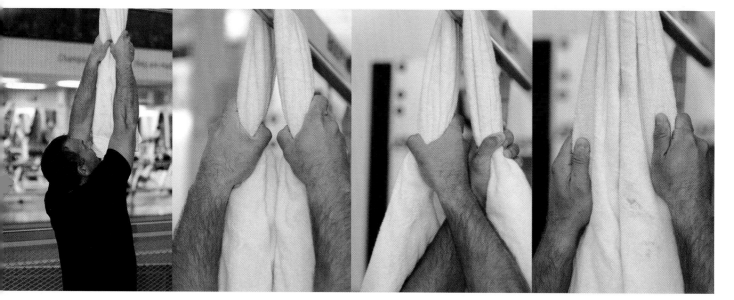

12. TOWEL CHIN-UP (PISTOL GRIP, CROSS GRIP, SLEEVE GRIP)

This classic exercise is very sport specific to Jiu Jitsu. Here the athlete performs pull-ups using identical grips found during a Jiu Jitsu match. If these become too easy, an athlete can add weight while these are performed.

13. GI CHIN-UP (PISTOL GRIP, CROSS GRIP, SLEEVE GRIP)

Begin by grasping the towel in one of the grip versions, as shown.
Pull the chest up to the bar, and lower under control.

Andre Gusmao and his opponent are in a battle of grips and arm strength during a submission attack.

Jay Heiron enlists his arms and grip to trap the arm of his opponent and look for the takedown.

Antonio McKee activates every muscle of his entire back to fight off the attack of Gabe Rivas.

ten

WARRIOR BACK TRAINING

A **warrior cannot control his opponent if he is pushing him away.** Even though a warrior may be hitting the gym hard, that warrior's training methods in the gym may not match the demands of actual competition in the ring. One of the most common errors in upper-body training is the overuse of *pushing* versus *pulling* movements used in training for fighting. Like a stiff upper cut to the jaw, this chapter is going to hammer home the need of pulling strength for the warrior athlete.

MMA has developed into a system that often involves pulling an opponent into a clinch, taking the opponent down by keeping them close, and then keeping him off balance, controlling and possibly submitting him with pulling movements on the ground. In everything from all takedown attempts like the double leg and arm drag to your opponent trying to get away or establish posture, you must be constantly using strong, continuous pulling movements. Even as an opponent drives into your guard or shoots in, or you snatch down on a guillotine for the finish, pulling is still more important than pushing an opponent away, to create off-balancing and control. The arms assist the warrior in these motions, but it is the large and powerful muscles of the back that make everything happen. This is why the warrior must have a chiseled back resembling a bag of rocks under his training shirt. Develop this critical area and you will have the edge over an opponent who focuses solely on upper-body pushing movements in the gym.

The pull-up and chin-up are probably two of the oldest known exercises. These are awesome exercises for the development of the muscles of the back, arms, and grip. The pull-up is also a great exercise for identifying relative body strength. This means how strong a warrior is at his or her body weight. Since most MMA events utilize weight classes, your goal as a warrior is to be the strongest competitor pound for pound in your weight division. Whether you are light or heavy, you need to be able to perform many pull-ups. Our gold standard for warriors is at least 20 pull-ups for a maximal attempt. If you cannot do 20, you need to either lose weight or get stronger at your current weight. This chapter is a comprehensive examination of the chin-up and pull-up, but make no mistake, fighters cannot live on chins alone.

There are many other exciting exercises in this chapter that stimulate the all-important warrior pulling strength. These exercises are designed to create pulling strength in all the directions needed for today's mixed martial artist. For you to really get the most out of your training, there has to be variety in not only the exercises but also in the directions of the movements.

The warrior back exercises in this chapter are going to help take every warrior's pulling strength to the next level. Examine its importance in MMA and how you can better work it into your own training. The time is now to add pulling strength to your training arsenal. Soon you will be going for arm drags and actually dragging the arm of your opponent right off!

BACK EXERCISES

1. FORWARD BODY PULL

Begin by lying on the stomach with the arms stretched out front.

Drive the arms and elbows into the ground and pull the body forward.

Once the hips are pulled toward the elbows, repeat for required distance.

2. PARTNER ROW

Begin by lying on the back, holding the wrists or hands of the partner straddled over you.

Keep the back flat and pull the body off the floor using only the heels (or the hips if heels are not possible) as a fulcrum.

Lower under control.

3. TWISTING TURTLE PICK-UP

Grasp around the waist of the partner, who is holding the turtle position on the floor.

Pick the turtle up and rotate him in the air (the turtle holds the position tight).

Place the turtle down facing the opposite direction from where you started.

4. PARTNER SWING

Begin standing, holding the partner around the waist, and sit his right hip on your left, as shown.

Lean back and swing the partner around your body so that his left hip lands on your right.

Repeat on both sides of the body.

5. PARTNER SCARECROW DRILL

Begin hanging from the standing partner's back, as shown.

Grasp under the partner's arm, and rotate your body around his.

Work your way around the standing partner back to the original position.

6. PARTNER FLIP

Begin with your arms clasped around the waist of the partner, who is on all fours.

Lift the partner upside down, and rotate his body to the other side of yours.

Place the partner down on all fours on the opposite side and repeat.

7. PARTNER PICK-UP

Partner #1 and #2 stand facing each other.

Partner #1 drops his level and puts his shoulder into #2's hip while grabbing behind his legs.

Partner #1 then stands up with #2 on his shoulder.

Partner #1 then lowers #2 under control and repeats on both sides.

8. CHIN-UP

Begin by grabbing the bar with both palms facing you, as shown.

Pull the body up to chest height, and lower under control.

9. ALTERNATE-GRIP PULL-UP

Begin by grabbing the bar with one hand pronated and one supinated, as shown.

Pull the body up to the bar to chest height, and lower under control.

10. NARROW-GRIP PULL-UP

Begin by placing the thumbs and index fingers next to
each other on the bar, as shown.

Pull the body up to the bar to chest height, and lower
under control.

11. WRIST/FOREARM-GRIP CHIN-UP

Begin by grabbing the wrist of the arm that is holding
the bar, as shown.

Pull the body up to the bar to chest height, and lower
under control.

12. NEUTRAL-GRIP PULL-UP

Begin by placing the hands on the bar attachment in the neutral position, as shown.

Pull the body up to the bar to chest height, and lower under control.

13. V-HANDLE NARROW PULL-UP

Begin by hanging from a V handle, which is usually used for rowing movements over the chin-up bar.

Pull the head up to one side of the bar, and lower under control.

Repeat by pulling the head up to the other side of the bar.

14. WIDE-GRIP PULL-UP

Begin by placing the hands on the bar farther than shoulder-width apart, as shown.

Pull the body up to the bar to chest height, and lower under control.

15. WIDE-GRIP BEHIND-THE-NECK PULL-UP

Begin by placing the hands on the bar farther than shoulder-width apart, as shown.

Pull the back of the neck up to the bar, and lower under control.

16. WIDE-GRIP CHIN-TO-HAND PULL-UP

Begin by placing the hands on the bar farther than shoulder-width apart, as shown.

Pull the body up to the bar to chest height, bring the chin to one hand, and return to the
  middle of the bar.

Lower under control; repeat and bring chin to the opposite hand.

17. POLE-VAULTER PULL-UP

Begin with a narrow pull-up grip on the bar, as shown.

Pull the knees to the chest and bring the feet up over the bar so that you are hanging upside down.

Pull the chest up to the bar, and then slowly lower the legs with knees straight as possible back to the starting point.

18. RENZO GRACIE PULL-UP

This version was first shown to me be Renzo Gracie, who banged out 30 reps of this without cracking a sweat!

Begin with a narrow pull-up grip on the bar, as shown.

After pulling the chest to the bar and having the knees pulled up, push yourself away from the bar by extending at the elbow, but keeping yourself at the same height.

Pull yourself back to the bar and repeat.

19. WEIGHTED-BELT PULL-UP/CHIN-UP

Once you are getting great at pull-ups and chin-ups (15–20 reps), it is time to add weight.
Start using a weight belt or vest and add enough weight to limit yourself to 5 reps. Perform
3 to 5 sets here, and try to raise the weight each week. The goal should be 100 added
pounds or more. A supertest of eccentric strength is what we call the **Negative Chin-up**.
Here we load the athlete with 100–200 pounds of extra weight and start him in the up
position. From there, the athlete lowers himself for 5–10 seconds under control. This
stimulates the recruitment of muscle that is rarely used.

Begin with the hands in the chin-up position, as shown, and a weight around the waist.
Pull the chest up to the bar, and lower under control.

20. STANDING HYPEREXTENSION

Begin with the feet hooked in the hyperextension machine with the upper body bent 90
  degrees at the waist, as shown.
Raise the torso to parallel with the body, and hold.
Lower the torso under control and repeat.

21. LOW BACK ON GLUTE-HAM

Begin hanging in the glute-ham machine with the torso at 45 degrees, as shown.

Raise the shoulders under control so that the body is in a straight line.

Slowly lower under control and repeat.

22. GLUTE-HAM RAISE

Begin with the feet hooked in the glute-ham machine and the upper body bent 90 degrees at the waist, as shown.

Raise the torso to parallel with the body, and then raise the entire body up from the knees.

Lower under control in the exact reverse order, and repeat for the required repetitions.

23. REVERSE HYPER (LEG VERSION)

This is an exercise that though you may not have the exact machine to perform it, you can do almost anywhere. If you have a reverse hyperextension machine available, you can add weight and perform the motion below.

To perform it on a regular high table, lie with the chest and stomach on the table and the legs hanging off one side.
Raise the legs parallel with the body, and hold for 8–10 seconds.

24. ROLLING THUNDER DEAD LIFT

This exercise requires two high boxes and a weight that can be lifted from the floor (we use a Rolling Thunder dead lift handle).

Begin by holding one hand tightly behind the back while the other holds the bar.
Squat down fully with the hips open to stretch the groin.
Stand up from the squat, holding the weight tight.
Lower under control and repeat.

25. SINGLE-ARM DEAD LIFT

Begin in the squat position, holding a bar in one hand, as shown.

Stand up by extending the knees, hips, and low back while maintaining a level posture.

Hold for 3 seconds at the top position, and then lower under control.

26. DECLINE DUMBBELL PULLOVER

This is the traditional bar pull-over exercise with a twist. By performing this exercise on a decline bench, the athlete travels through a fuller range of motion with resistance on the muscles.

Begin on the back with dumbbell held over the chest, as shown. Reach all the way back with the elbows slightly bent.

Return the bar to the original position.

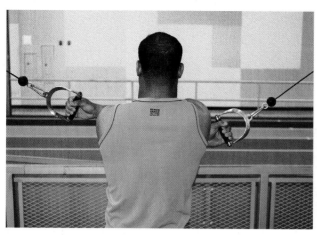

27. REVERSE CABLE FLY

Use a high cable or a cable that is at the same height as the chest. Stand in between the columns after grabbing the cables on the opposite side of each arm so that the arms are crossed over the body, as shown.

Extend at the shoulders and elbows, and drive the cables out at the sides.
Lower under control.

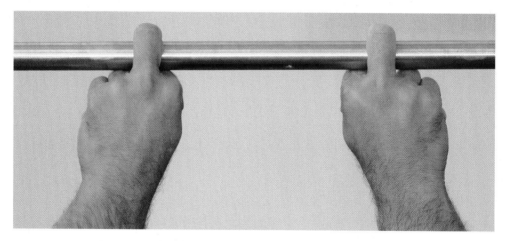

28. DECREASED FINGER CHIN-UP

In this exercise, the athlete is forced to use fewer fingers on the bar. I usually take fingers off the bar starting from the little finger, then the ring finger, leaving the middle and index on the bar. The ultimate challenge is the middle-finger chin-up. Although most athletes can't even hold their own weight from there, I have seen athletes do such chin-ups for five reps. Attempt that one with EXTREME CAUTION.

Begin with fewer fingers on the bar, as shown.
Pull the chest up to the bar, and lower under control.

Delson Heleno utilizes his back muscles to help deliver strikes to his opponent.

Matt Horwich contracts his back muscles to pull Ryan McGivern in for a takedown attempt.

Cam Ward demonstrates how the abdominal muscles are
involved in delivering a powerful punch.

eleven

WARRIOR ABDOMINAL TRAINING

A warrior can have strong arms and strong legs, but if he is soft in the middle, he will probably not be a warrior for long. The abdominal region of the body is an essential area that allows the powerful forces that are transmitted through the feet and up the legs of the warrior to then pass on through to the upper body for devastating throws, slams, and punches. The abdominals are also critical for the force and speed displayed with brutal leg, body, and head kicks. On the ground, the abs are important for keeping posture when the warrior is either in the guard position or on top searching for submissions. Without proper abdominal development, the warrior is leaving his or her midsection, and the chance for defeat, wide open.

A common mistake for a warrior is believing that working just a little bit of abdominal training into a workout will be enough to develop a set of bulletproof abs. Another mistake is thinking that these muscles respond only to high repetitions. A final common error is just performing exercises that move in only one plane of motion, such as the classic sit-up or crunch.

The exercises in this chapter are going to smash these old ways of thinking right in the teeth. As the warrior will see from the workouts at the end of this book, he or she must devote considerably more time to abdominal work than the classic last-five-minutes following training. The warrior will also see from the exercises in this chapter that abdominal exercises must occur in multiple planes and directions to truly prepare this region of the body for war. The warrior will also be enlightened to the fact that to truly make this region strong, you must train with heavy resistance, just as with every other muscle of the warrior's body. These exercises will force warriors to take their abdominal work out of the Stone Age and into the future of MMA training.

If you are a warrior looking for that set of six-pack abs, remember that everyone has a set of abs; they just might not be visible because of what is covering them up. The ability to clean a pair of fight shorts across your washboard stomach is going to depend on your attention to both physical training and nutrition. The exercises in this chapter are one part of the two-part methodology for having a great set of abs. The other is proper diet. Information on nutrition to achieve the rock-hard warrior look is contained in the "Warrior Performance Nutrition" chapter.

ABDOMINAL EXERCISES

1. ABDOMINAL BACKWARD SLIDE

Begin by sitting with the hands at the sides.

Lift the buttocks off the ground, and slide it backward as far as possible.

Lower body under control, and repeat for required distance.

2. PIKE-UP

Begin by lying on the back, with the legs extended and the arms held overhead.

Raise the legs and the arms so that the hands and the toes meet over the body.

Lower under control while keeping the back flat.

Repeat for the required number of repetitions.

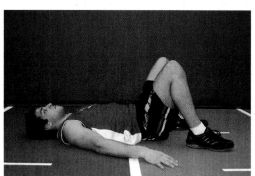

3. TRIANGLE HIP RAISE

Begin by lying on the back, with the arms extended at the sides and the palms down.

Raise the hips up into the air and cross the legs in the triangle position.

Lower under control while uncrossing the legs, and return to the original position.

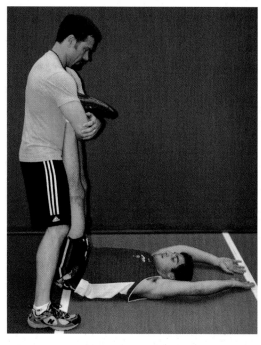

4. PARTNER PIKE-UP

One partner begins by standing over the supine partner, holding that partner's legs
  extended from the ankles, as shown.

The partner on his back then reaches up with his hands in attempt to grasp his toes.

That partner then lowers back down to the ground.

5. PARTNER LEG THROW

One partner begins by lying on his back while grasping the ankles of the partner
standing over him, as shown.

The supine partner kicks his extended legs up toward the standing partner's hands.

The standing partner receives the feet and quickly throws them back to the ground,
either forward or to the side.

The supine partner slows the legs under control, returns to start position, and repeats
for the required number of repetitions.

6. PARTNER HIP EXCHANGE

The partners begin by lying side by side, with heads in the opposite direction and
the knees bent, as shown.

Each partners extends an arm under the bent knees of the other and they clasp
hands, as shown.

The partners then lift hips under control and exchanges the position of the hips,
as shown.

7A. MED-BALL TOE TOUCH

Begin by lying on the back, with the med ball on the chest and the toes in the air.

Extend the hands with the ball toward the toes, lifting the torso off the ground.

Lower under control and repeat.

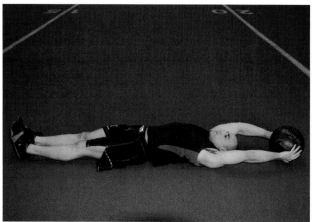 

7B. MED-BALL PIKE-UP

Begin by lying on the back, with the legs straight and the arms extended with the med ball
  over the head.

Raise the straight legs and arms into the air to meet above the body.

Lower the legs and arms slowly under control, keeping the back flat on the floor.

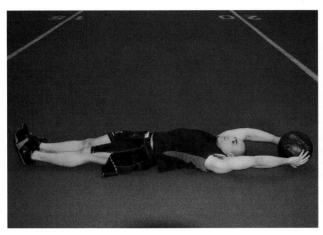 

8. MED-BALL SINGLE-LEG KICK

Begin by lying on the back, with the legs straight and the arms extended with the med ball over the head.

Raise one straight leg to meet the arms with the ball in the air above the body.

Lower the leg and arms slowly under control, keeping the back flat on the floor.

Perform this on both sides and repeat.

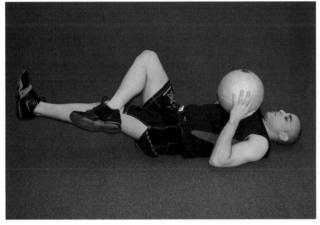 

9. MED-BALL TRIANGLE CRUNCH

Begin on the back, holding the med ball on the chest and with the legs crossed in the triangle position, as shown.

Keep the lower leg straight, but do not let it touch the floor.

Bring the lower leg's knee up as high as possible, and crunch the upper body forward.

Lower under control and repeat.

10. MED-BALL EXPLOSIVE SIT-UP

Begin on the back, with the knees bent and the med ball held overhead.

Bring the ball to the chest and sit up as fast as possible.

In the sitting position, press the med ball toward the ceiling.

Return back to the original position under control and repeat.

11. PARTNER MED-BALL EXCHANGE

The partners begin by lying on their backs, with the knees bent and their ankles interlocked, as shown.

The partners sit up together, and one passes the ball to the other.

The partners lower back to the original position, and then sit up again and exchange the ball again.

12. MED-BALL FIGURE 8 DRILL

Begin by sitting on the buttocks, holding the feet in the air and with the med ball in
   one hand.

Raise one leg and bend at the knee while the other leg is held off the floor.

Pass the ball under the raised knee and over the lower leg.

Now raise the opposite knee, and repeat the exercise on the other side.

13. PHYSIOBALL EXCHANGE

Begin by lying on the back, with the legs extended and the physioball held overhead.

Raise the legs and place the physioball in between the feet, and then lower the legs and arms back to the original position.

Repeat the motion and place the ball back in the hands.

14. PHYSIOBALL KNEE TUCK

Begin with the knees placed on the ball and the hands placed on the ground, as shown.

Extend at the knees and the hips into the push-up position.

Return the knees forward back to the original position.

15A. SIDE STABILITY HOLD

Begin on your side, propped on an elbow.

Lift the hips from the floor so that you are supported by only the side of the bottom foot and the elbow.

Hold this position for 20 seconds.

15B. ABDUCTED SIDE STABILITY HOLD

Begin on your side, propped on an elbow, with the other arm at 90 degrees to the body.

Lift the hips from the floor; this time you also lift up the top leg at a 45-degree angle from the body.

Hold this position for 20 seconds.

16A. PRONE ABDOMINAL PLANK

Begin on the stomach, with the body propped up on the elbows and toes, as shown.

Lift the hips and round the upper back while keeping the abs as tight as possible.

Hold for 20 seconds.

16B. SINGLE-LEG PRONE ABDOMINAL PLANK

Begin on the stomach with the body propped up on the elbows and toes, as shown.

Lift one leg from the floor while keeping the abs as tight as possible.

Hold for 20 seconds.

17. ABDOMINAL PLANK PRESS

Begin on the stomach, with the arms stretched out overhead.

Press into the ground with the palms and toes and lift the body off the ground.

Hold this plank position for 10 seconds.

18. PARTNER SHRIMP DRILL

Begin by lying on one side between the standing partner's legs.

Place the hands on the standing partner's shin.

Push with hands and slide your hips through and away from the partner.

19. PARTNER ABDOMINAL SIT-UP

Begin with the legs interlocked around the waist of the standing partner.

Lower your torso as much as possible.

Return to the original position by using the abs to sit up.

20. PARTNER SEESAW SIT-UP

Your partner begins in the pike position, with you sitting on your partner's shoulders with your legs hooked on your partner's thighs.

The sitting partner lowers the torso, while the prone partner balances on the forearms.

The sitting partner returns to the original position.

21A. PARTNER PUSH-UP AB DRILL

Your partner begins in the push-up position, with you sitting on your partner's shoulders
with your legs hooked on your partner's thighs.

The sitting partner leans back and lowers the torso as far as possible.

The sitting partner returns to the original position.

21B. PARTNER ALL-FOURS AB DRILL

Your partner begins on hands and knees, with you sitting on your partner's shoulders with
your legs hooked on your partner's thighs.

The sitting partner leans back and lowers the torso as far as possible.

The sitting partner returns to the original position.

22. OLYMPIC-BAR TWIST

Begin with the bar held out front overhead with the arms outstretched.

Move in a circular pattern to the right while keeping the hips and feet forward.

Bring the bar back up to the starting position, and move now to the other side.

23. OLYMPIC-BAR BUS DRIVER

Begin in the same position as for the bar twist, but this time hold the plate at the edges.

Move in a circular pattern to the right while keeping the hips and feet forward.

Bring the weight back up to the starting position, and switch to the other side.

24. OLYMPIC-BAR ONE-HAND SNATCH

Begin by placing a nonweighted end of an Olympic bar in a corner or against a solid
foundation that will not allow it to slip.

Then weight the other end accordingly, and move to that end of the bar.

Face perpendicular to the bar.

Squat down and grasp the open end of the bar with the left hand.

Use the legs and core to quickly stand and snatch the bar up to an extended position.

Slowly return it down to the floor and repeat.

25. OLYMPIC-BAR PUNCH

This exercise can be used as a continuation of
the One-Hand Snatch or by itself.

In the finished snatch position from the One-
Hand Snatch, the athlete is facing the bar
with the arm with the bar held overhead.

Lower that hand to the shoulder.

Using the arms and legs, punch the arm
forward and up.

Return the hand to the shoulder and repeat.

26. CABLE AND PHYSIOBALL SIDE TWIST

Begin by standing with your feet and hips facing perpendicular to the cable column, with your left shoulder closest to the column.

Cradle the physioball between your arms and against your chest, and twist the shoulders to the left so you can grasp the handle.

Make sure you are far enough away from the column to get a full stretch.

While maintaining your hip and foot position, now twist all the way to your right.

Return slowly and under control and repeat.

27. CABLE AND PHYSIOBALL DOWNWARD TWIST

Place the handle at the highest position on the cable column.

Begin in the same position as for the side twist.

While maintaining your hip and foot position, now twist all the way down and diagonal to your right.

Return up slowly and under control and repeat.

28. CABLE AND PHYSIOBALL UPWARD TWIST

Place the handle at the lowest position on the cable column.

Begin in the same position as for the side twist.

While maintaining your hip and foot position, now twist all the way up and diagonal to your right.

Return down slowly and under control, and repeat.

29. CABLE AND PHYSIOBALL SUPLEX

Place the handle at the lowest position on the cable column.

Face the cable column in the squat position, with the arm of the hand holding the handle reaching over the top of the ball.

While maintaining your hip and foot position and while looking over one shoulder, now lift the ball all the way up by extending the back and hips.

Return down and squat slowly and under control and repeat.

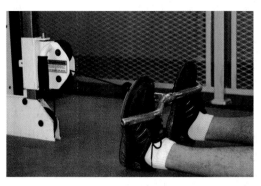 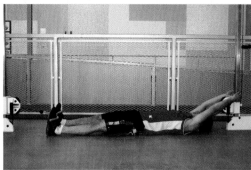 

30. CABLE HIP-FLEXOR PULL (KNEE TUCK)

Begin on the back, with the hands holding the body in a stable position.

The bar from the cable is held by keeping the toes pulled up.

Bring the knees up as high as possible while trying to maintain a flat back against
the ground.

Return under control and repeat.

31. SINGLE-ARM DUMBBELL SIDE BEND

Begin by standing with a dumbbell held in one hand while maintaining the shoulders in a
level position.

Lower the dumbbell by bending to that side, and then return to original level position.

32. OVERHEAD DUMBBELL SIDE BEND

Begin by holding the dumbbells in each hand overhead.

Bend directly to the side, keeping the arms held straight overhead and maintaining the distance between of the dumbbells.

Return to the starting position, and bend to the other side.

33. UNILATERAL SIDE BEND

Stand with an unevenly weighted bar and assume the level position, as if the bar were equally weighted.

Bend as far to the side as possible at the waist, and return to the level position.

Repeat for the required number of repetitions, and perform on the other side.

34. BOXER'S DUMBBELL SPEED TWIST

Begin by sitting on the floor with your feet in the air balancing only on the buttocks.

Hold a dumbbell in front with both hands.

Begin twisting side to side as fast as possible.

Keep the feet in the air for the whole set and make sure that the shoulders are twisting and not just the arms.

35. KNEELING FORWARD BAR ROLL

Start on the knees, with the hands on the bar at shoulder-width apart.

Roll the bar forward on the ground while keeping the arms and low back straight.

Roll the bar out until the body is horizontal, and then return to kneeling by contracting the abs.

36. STANDING FORWARD BAR ROLL

Start by standing with the hands on the bar at shoulder-width apart.

Roll the bar forward on the ground while keeping the arms and low back straight.

Roll the bar out until the body is horizontal, and then return to standing by contracting the abs.

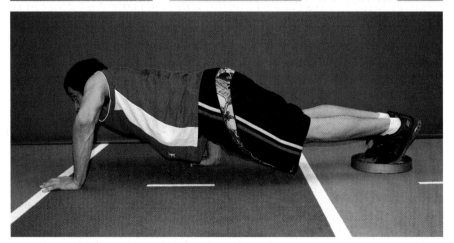

37. ALLIGATOR CRAWL

Start in a push-up position, with the toes placed on an object that will slide with some resistance on the floor (25-pound plate, Frisbee, etc.).

From this position, "walk" the required distance on the hands, both forward and backward.

This can be done slowly or for speed.

Keep the back flat and repeat.

Ryan Schultz uses his abdominals to attempt to control Joe Sampieri on the ground.

This photo demonstrates that the abdominals are important in both submission attempts and escape.

Renzo Gracie's guillotine places Pat Miletich in a position of high energy expenditure.

twelve

WARRIOR HEART AND LUNG TRAINING

A **warrior must never let cardiovascular fatigue be the reason for defeat.** It has been said that fatigue makes cowards of us all. No matter how strong, fast, or technically proficient a warrior is, if that warrior is dead tired, that warrior is vulnerable. Though a warrior can build fitness during technical training, specifically gearing training to develop endurance is critical to eventual victory. This should tell every warrior that the heart is as important as, if not more important than, any other muscle in the body. Training this muscle must occur if the warrior is ever to reach full potential.

A warrior must understand that everything in life is cyclical. Whether it is day to night, birth to death, or the increase and decrease of the heart rate during the rounds of a fight, everything is cyclical. Knowing this, the warrior will understand that the endurance training for mixed martial arts must mimic the cycle of the fight in order to properly prepare the energy systems of the body for battle.

In this chapter, I describe what has come to be known in our preparation as *hurricane training*. A hurricane is a powerful yet brief storm that leaves destruction in its wake that then calls for renewal and rebuilding. The effect of our cardiovascular-fitness training on the warrior's body and mind mimics this. These training sessions are intense yet brief and often replicate the exact demands of an MMA match. As a result, over time, the warrior will develop not only the endurance to go the distance but also the most important characteristic that a warrior must have, the ability to control the mind when the going gets tough.

There are many ways that the hurricane can be replicated in training. We use a variety of tools to achieve our results. The hurricane is measured on a category scale in which category 1 is the easiest and category 5 is the most difficult. Once a warrior understands the concept of hurricane training and how to measure the level of intensity for the workout, the warrior can pick and choose the different modalities contained in this chapter to add variety and excitement to training. In the "Warrior Workouts" chapter, there are many examples of specific hurricane training regimes.

Weights make it easy for a warrior to determine if he or she is making progress during strength training. For cardiovascular development, however, it is not as easy for the warrior to monitor progress. Because of this fact, I recommend that every warrior use a heart-rate monitor during this style of training. Without this biofeedback, the warrior is training as blindly as if he or she were wearing a blindfold during weight work. Without this information, the intensity of the workouts and the warrior's progress overtime can't be measured.

This will be the most difficult yet rewarding training that you can perform. A warrior must learn to push beyond the pain of fatigue to eventually become not only more physically fit, but also mentally tough. Only when this occurs can one consider oneself a true warrior.

THE HISTORY OF THE HURRICANE

A common mistake made by athletes and trainers is to focus their training solely on what they are good at or what they enjoy most. When I began training fighters and training in the martial arts, I was no exception. At the time I began this training, over a decade ago, I was very strong, but surely did not have the stamina to match the strength or the endurance needed to be a world-class fighter. Instead of training myself and my fighters to improve our endurance specifically for the energy-system training that was required for their sport, I blindly continued to concentrate on the overall strength of my athletes. As a result, although our athletes were winning world titles and matches at the UFC and PRIDE (PRIDE Fighting Championships), I began to see that their cardiovascular conditioning was becoming a limiting factor.

After one of my athletes suffered a loss for lack of cardiovascular conditioning, I challenged my thought process about our physical preparation. I realized that the enemy of becoming the best at something was simply *being good at something else to start with*. I began to realize that getting great at your weaknesses and making them your strengths was a key to both physical and personal growth. This new way of thinking forced me to concentrate on the two most important pieces of anatomy in fight training: the brain and the heart. That is when I started creating what I call *hurricane training*.

When you start getting into this style of training, or start to surround yourself with people that enjoy this style of training, you see nothing but gluttons for punishment. Hard anaerobic work for 5-to-10-minute bursts is nothing short of a form of self-torture at first. As my athletes and others involved in this style of training will say though, once you get used to this type of work, it really becomes a form of enlightenment. This style of training will teach you more about yourself than lifting or sprinting. This type of training tells you who you are, what is important to you, and how skillful you are at pushing yourself to the limit. I say *skillful* because I have learned that it is not an innate ability, as I originally thought; it is, in fact, a skill.

When I started the circuits with myself and the athletes, we always began on the conservative side. As our bodies, hearts, and minds got tougher, however, we started to see how far we could actually push on the first attempt of something. This ability to attack and go through pain to learn about what we were doing to ourselves was another step in our enlightenment.

The circuits started with combinations of ladder drills, hurdle drills, box jumps, and med-ball work. We had stations set up, and performed the prescribed number of reps at each station until the set time had elapsed. If we were doing multiple sets, we would then attempt to beat the original volume of work in the same amount of time (this is always much tougher than it sounds). After this, we started working on high-speed treadmills and interspersing exercises between the sets. From there, we incorporated sparring or bag work with the sprints, as well. It was around that time that things started to really heat up, as we tested the true limits of our bodies.

For over a year, we experimented with this level of training and kept manipulating the sprint time (from 6 to eventually 30 seconds); the exercises, reps, and sets per circuit; and the time frame that an actual circuit could last. After this, the most devastating circuits began to be created. With years of experimenting and training under our belts, each session became a test to see how far we could go. Enter the strongman circuits and the hurricane analogy.

A number of months before the writing of this, we purchased a few new pieces of equipment that were "strongman" in nature. When I write "strongman," I am talking about exercises like the giant tire, farmer's walk, sandbag carry, thick-rope-pull drags, heavy sled or car pulls, and the like from television fame. We had used a number of these pieces on a separate training day from that of the endurance work, but the group was ready for a new challenge. That is how we created the *category 5 hurricane*. We started performing these sessions every Tuesday at the facility, and it was the one day of the week I looked forward to and dreaded at the same time. At the end of the sessions, the group would always sit, recover, and talk about fighting, philosophy, or whatever was on the national scene. After one particularly tough session (and they are always tough), World Champion Grappler Roger Gracie stated that he felt as if he had just been hit by a hurricane, "and it was no category 1 or 2, it was a category 5, baby!" Right then, we all understood, and we started to classify the level we took a session to by the 1–5 hurricane category scale. After looking over my progression with these sessions over the years, I have broken down this style of training into five categories that can be completed over 12 weeks.

CATEGORY 1

Indications

This style of training is used as the introduction to huricane circuits for beginner athletes with little experience in the area. This can also be used as a recovery session if you back down the intensity after overtraining or coming off a competition.

Methods

For this method, I use the high-speed treadmill alone with 10-second sprints at a low to moderate intensity. Your heart rate is monitored, and after each rep on the tread, your heart rate (HR) must return to 120 beats per minute (BPM) before you get back on the tread for another sprint. This way, you can do 6–10 sets comfortably with little fear of nausea. The rest periods should be timed and recorded, with the goal of each subsequent training session being to have less recovery time per set.

Time Frames

You should perform this style of training for the first few weeks (2–3) of training.

Sample Circuit

Treadmill at 9–10 mph and 10% grade for sets of 10 sec., with adequate recovery to reach 120 BPM.

CATEGORY 2

Indications

As your recovery time improves, abdominal med-ball exercises are now introduced during what was the recovery portion between the sprints. The sprints can be also taken up to 12–15 seconds.

Methods

For this method, I use a number of different weighted med balls and perform 3 sets of 2 different ab exercises after the first 3 sprints. Then I choose 2 new exercises for the next 3 sets, and then 2 final exercises for the last 3 sets, to equal 9 total sprints and 18 sets of abs. The speed can increase every 3rd set on the treadmill. All of the sets are performed as quickly as possible. HR can still be monitored, but 120 is not required to start the next set.

Time Frames

This style of training can be performed for the next 2 weeks of training.

Sample Circuit

Treadmill at 9 mph and 10% grade for 20 sec. for 3 sets with Med-Ball Toe Touch (pg 138) 10 reps and Med-Ball Pike Up (pg 138) 8 reps after each sprint.

Treadmill at 10 mph and 10% grade for 20 sec. for 3 sets with Boxer's Dumbbell Speed Twist (pg 154) 50 reps after each sprint.

Treadmill at 11 mph and 10% grade for 20 sec. for 3 sets with Med-Ball Triangle Crunch (pg 139) 12 reps on each leg after each sprint.

CATEGORY 3
Indications
The abdominals should now be tolerable, and sparring exercises (boxing, muay thai, pummeling) are now introduced for a specific time frame between the sprints. The sprints are now 15–18 seconds.

Methods
For this method, I have my fighters do 10 "rounds" between the treadmill and pad work, with a partner next to the treadmill. The sparring aspect of the training should be 1 minute in length between sprints, and each round should have a particular focus from the person holding the pads. This is all now performed continuously, with no rest.

Time Frames
At about 5–6 weeks into the training, the athlete can start to experiment here, or he can move to a lower version of category 4.

Sample Circuit
Treadmill at 10 mph and 10% grade for 18 sec., with 1 minute of sparring for 9 sets (total time of the circuit is 15 min.).

CATEGORY 4

Indications

Now you are prepared to tolerate higher intensity levels and your mind is strong. At this time free weights are introduced into the period between the sprints. The sprints are now 20 seconds.

Methods

For this method we again perform 3 blocks of 3 sets of sprints with 2 different exercises in each set. For each sprint, the speed will now increase. The intensity of the weight will determine the overall difficulty of the circuit. The rule of thumb is to start with 30%–50% of your maximum weight on the exercises and perform 8–10 reps on each.

Time Frames

This is reserved for about 7–8 weeks into your training cycle.

Sample Circuit

Treadmill at 9, 9.5, and 10 mph and 10% grade for 25 sec. for 3 sets with Close-Grip Bench Press (pg 92) 8 reps and Chin-ups (pg 92) 8 reps after each sprint.

Treadmill at 10.5, 11, and 11.5 mph and 10% grade for 25 sec. for 3 sets with Weighted Dip (pg 93) 10 reps and Band Curls (pg 110) 10 reps after each sprint.

Treadmill at 12, 13, and 14 mph and 10% grade for 20 sec. for 3 sets with Tire Flip (pg 107) 10 flips after each sprint.

CATEGORY 5

Indications

This is reserved for the athletes with the highest level of intensity tolerance and who have no major competitions for a few weeks. Now strongman, full-body activities are introduced into the period between sprints. The sprints are now 20 or more seconds.

Methods

For this method we again perform 3 blocks of 3 sets of sprints with 2 different exercises in each set. For each sprint, the speed will now increase. The intensity of the strongman exercise will determine the overall difficulty of the circuit.

Time Frames

This is performed at 9–12 weeks into your training.

Sample Circuit

Treadmill at 9, 9.5, and 10 mph and 10% grade for 30 sec. for 3 sets with Arm-over-Arm Rope Pull (pg 108) 40 yards and Farmer's Walk (pg 106) 40 yards after each spring.

Treadmill at 10.5, 11, and 11.5 mph and 10% grade for 25 sec. for 3 sets with Tire Flip (pg 107) 10 flips after each sprint.

Treadmill at 12, 13, and 14 mph and 10% grade for 20 sec. for 3 sets with Sandbag Pick-up (pg 109) 10 pick ups after each spring.

When a hurricane passes through your area, things are never the same. Often, its effects are long lasting and something that people do not soon forget. To anyone that dares to go into the eye of the category 5 that I have described here, if you find that it is peaceful, it is because you have actually passed out. But after these 12 weeks of training, you will be physically and mentally stronger than ever before.

USE OF A HEART-RATE MONITOR

For the last number of years, this hurricane training has served us well, but as with anything else, I am always trying to improve what we are doing. I was trying to discover how to keep the mind under control even when the athlete is under great physical stress during these hurricane sessions. I realized that since the athlete had no reference point, in terms of biofeedback, for this style of training, it was difficult for the athlete to manage or determine the level of progress or overall conditioning. In weightlifting, it's easy to determine if an athlete is getting stronger by the change in weights or to determine the intensity of any workout from the amount of weight used. For cardiovascular training, however, this was much more difficult.

If you never had a speedometer in your car, how would you know what 55 mph "felt" like? It was only through the practice of looking at the speedometer and matching the velocity with your experience that you learned what 55 felt like and then began to understand how fast you were moving at a certain "feel." The same is true for heart rate. If you don't know what it "feels" like when your heart is at 170 beats per minute or you cannot match an intensity level with this rate, you are essentially exercising as blindly as you would be driving a car without a speedometer. In every session, whether it is running or lifting, my athletes now wear monitors, not only to let me know their status at any time during the session, but also so that they can develop a sensitivity that connects their heart rate and their mind, to better understand themselves. This is known as biofeedback, and it is critical for an athlete in order to better understand his or her own body and how it responds to and, as you will see in the next paragraph, recovers from bouts of exercise.

The most important recent discovery I have made in this type of training was finding out that heart-rate recovery was an important aspect of training I was not focusing on, and neither were my athletes. I realized that though it is important for fighters to be able to perform at a high heart rate and intensity, it is also important for the heart to be able to quickly recover. This is now known in science as heart-rate variability (HRV) and is becoming seen as a most important ability to work through progressive, cyclical training. HRV can be described simply as the capacity of the heart to recover and do work. Without this ability, if there are multiple rounds or fights in one day, the stage can be set for disaster. In our cyclical training, we monitor not only the maximum heart rate during activity, but also the speed at which the heart rate returns to our accepted value to tell us that the athlete has recovered. If you are not looking at and training this variable, you are doing only half the work.

If you do not have a heart-rate monitor or don't monitor this value in training, I suggest you get one. Without this information about yourself, every cardio session is essentially guesswork. Without the properly trained endurance, you can be the strongest, fastest athlete and still be in big trouble. Endurance is the key to success, and matching it with an understanding of mentally knowing at any moment where the body is and what it has left in the tank comes through trial-and-error work with your biofeedback. Recent research is identifying the critical moment in sport at which, even though one athlete may have more of such physical attributes as strength and explosiveness, an opponent that is better able to control his or her HR and recover may have a better opportunity to make the right decision at the right time. This ability can and does lead to success in combat sports all the time. Some may call it strategy or fight architecture, but now science is finding that the connection between the heart and mind plays a big role in victory.

In addition to monitoring physical training such as lifting and running, I think that monitoring fight-specific training will also be very important in the future of this sport. By better understanding the physical demands of certain positions and situations in a fight, coaches and athletes will better learn how to relax, improve technique, and control their bodies and emotions. Until we exactly understand the demands of this great sport, how can we ever adequately prepare ourselves for it?

To summarize, your training should be brief, cyclical, and mimic the demands of the actual sport. Every training session should be monitored, and you should be looking not only at the HR maximum but also at the heart's ability to recover, in terms of rate and time. This will create more time for overall recovery, prevent injury, and give you much better understanding. In the great scheme of training and the martial arts, that self-awareness is, after all, the ultimate goal.

HEART AND LUNG EXERCISES

Hammer

When using the hammer, make sure that you have an object that you are hitting that not only absorbs the force but also does not splinter or shatter. A rubber tire is a great option for this exercise, and most can be found for free.

1. OVERHEAD HAMMER STRIKE

Grasp the hammer at the end with the left hand and near the head with the right.
Face the horizontal tire, with the feet, hips, and shoulders forward.
Bring the hammer head back over the shoulder on the right side, up and behind the body.
Slide the left hand down to meet the right as you initiate the strike from overhead.
Finish the drill with a powerful strike, and repeat on the opposite side.

2. DIAGONAL HAMMER STRIKE

Grasp the hammer at the end with the left hand and at mid-shaft on the right.

Face the vertical tire, with the feet, hips, and shoulders forward.

Bring the hammer head straight back over the right shoulder.

Using the torso, strike the tire, keeping the hips and feet forward.

3. SIDE HAMMER STRIKE

Begin with a wide stance, holding the hammer with the hands far apart, as shown.

To strike, pull forward and downward with the left hand and push the right hand forward.

This action creates a pull across the torso of the athlete.

Keep the hips in a static position as this rotation of the upper body occurs.

4. KNEELING OVERHEAD HAMMER STRIKE

This is a great exercise for developing powerful strikes from the top position during groundwork.

Grasp the hammer at the end with the left hand and mid-shaft with the right.
Kneel facing the horizontal tire, with the hips and shoulders forward.
Bring the hammer head back on the right side, up and behind the body.
Slide the left hand down to meet the right as you initiate the strike from overhead.
Finish the drill with a powerful strike, and repeat on the opposite side.

Ladder (Lower Body)

1. SLALOM HOP

Begin at one end of the ladder, facing forward with one foot inside the ladder.

Hop side to side while traveling down the ladder.

With each jump there is a new lead foot in the ladder.

Keep the hips over the ladder as you move forward.

2. IN-AND-OUT FOOT HOP

Begin at one end of the ladder, with the feet on either side of it.

Hop forward, bringing both feet into the box, and then hop forward again, bringing both feet out on the side again.

Repeat this pattern as you move down the ladder.

3. MUHAMMAD ALI

Begin by standing at the side of the ladder, facing it.

Move the lead foot into a box, then quickly switch it with the other foot.

Switch the left and right foot in and out of each box as you travel down the ladder.

Use an opposite arm/leg movement.

4. HIP TWIST

Begin with one foot in the ladder, and the entire body facing forward.

Jump so that even though the upper body and shoulders are still facing forward, the hips and feet are now perpendicular to the shoulders and the other foot is in the ladder.

Jump to the next box and return the hips and feet to the original position.

Repeat for the entire ladder.

5. MUAY THAI KICK DEFENSE

Begin outside the ladder, facing forward, as shown.

Step into the ladder with the right foot, then into the ladder with the left, and then as you step out of the ladder with the right foot, the left knee and the arms are used in a muay thai kick defense position.

Use a 1-2-3 count on the drill.

6. ONE FOOT IN EACH BOX, RUNNING FORWARD

Begin outside the ladder, with the elbows held at 90 degrees.

Run in the ladder, stepping one foot in each box, bringing the knees up to 90 degrees.

Run through the entire ladder.

7. TWO FEET IN EACH BOX, SIDEWAYS

Begin outside the ladder, facing sideways.

Step each foot into each box as you move laterally down the ladder.

Keep the elbows at 90 degrees, and run through the entire ladder.

8. ONE-FOOT BUNNY HOP

Begin at one end of the ladder, standing on one foot.

Hop on only one foot in every box down the entire ladder.

Repeat with the other foot.

Plyo Box Jumps

1. HIGH-BOX FORWARD JUMP

Stand facing the box in the squat position.

Swing the arms down as fast as possible and back up to assist jump.

Jump up onto the box and land with soft feet by bending at the knees.

2. SINGLE-LEG HIGH-BOX FORWARD JUMP

Stand facing the box, squatting on only one leg.

Swing the arms down as fast as possible and back up to assist the jump.

Jump up onto the box from the one leg, and land softly on that foot.

3. TWISTING HIGH-BOX JUMP

Stand facing the box in the squat position.

Swing the arms down as fast as possible and back up to assist the jump.

When jumping, twist the body in the air, and land perpendicular to takeoff.

4. TWISTING SINGLE-LEG HIGH-BOX JUMP

Stand facing the box, squating on only one leg.

Swing the arms down as fast as possible and back up to assist the jump.

When jumping, twist the body in the air, and land perpendicular to take off on one foot.

Sled Exercises

The sled is one of the most infamous tools at my facility among the fighters. This piece is very versatile and can be used as a tool to achieve either speed, strength, or endurance.

1. SIDEWAYS SLED PULL

Begin sideways to the sled, holding the ropes around the waist, as shown.
Take crossover steps while keeping the feet and hips facing forward.
Continue for the required distance.

2. BACKWARD SLED PULL

Begin facing the sled, holding the ropes in the hands, as shown.
Take small backward steps using a toe-to-heel relationship while leaning slightly backward.
Continue for the required distance.

3. FORWARD SLED PULL

Begin with the back to the sled, holding the ropes in the hands, as shown.

Take as big a step forward as possible, staying on the balls of the feet while maintaining a 45-degree angle with the body.

Continue for the required distance.

4. FORWARD SLED PUSH

Begin with the hands on the sled or another pushable object (a car is possible), as shown.

Push into the sled and take as big a stride as possible, staying on the balls of the feet.

Continue for the required distance.

5. BAND-PUNCHING FORWARD SLED PULL

Begin with the back to the sled, holding the ropes around the waist and the band around the back in the hands, as shown.

Walk forward, and with each step punch with the arm opposite of the leg that steps forward.

Continue for the required distance.

6. BAND BACKWARD SLED PULL

Begin facing the sled, with the ropes tied around the waist and the band held in front of the body, as shown.

Begin to walk backward and pull the arms out to the sides, for 10 steps.

Bring the hands back together for 5 steps and repeat.

Continue for the required distance.

Bar Complex Training

When most warriors think about weight training, they think that the only use for bars and weights is to build strength. Many would also agree that loading the bar with as many iron plates as possible, until the bar is a mass of bending steel, is the only way to get stronger. On the other hand, if you ask many warriors out there today how to build endurance, they will probably tell you to go ride the stationary bike or jog on a treadmill. This section is going to show you how strength training can also build speed and strength endurance using very little weights or even no weight on the bar at all.

My team of warriors has enjoyed success with a training method called *bar complexes*. This style of training involves doing a *chain of exercises in a row with the same weight without stopping*. The goal of this training is to finish the prescribed exercise as fast as possible in order to improve strength, speed, and conditioning. This style of training is an excellent choice for warming up for lifting or training sessions, as well as during either preparatory or competition phases of training.

There are an infinite number of ways to utilize this technique. The methods can involve a bar or dumbbell. We prefer the bar for complex training. These methods can also involve any variety of exercise. This section demonstrates how we use the technique at our facility. We perform 5 sets of bar complexes as our warm-ups for our workouts, and use *time per set* as the indicator for how much weight should be placed on the bar. For instance, we begin with the empty 45-pound bar and perform the first set of 12 exercises. Each exercise is performed for 6 repetitions without stopping and at maximal speed. The goal of the 12-exercise set is to finish the set in less than 1 minute. If this occurs, you then add 5 pounds for the second set. If you beat the time again, add another 5 pounds for the next set, and so on. If you do not beat 1 minute, you stay with the same weight and continue to attempt to beat that time. For some of our lighter athletes, it took a number of weeks of practice to move beyond just the bar. Remember that each repetition is performed as fast as possible, but that does not mean you are allowed to sacrifice technique. Still use as full a range of motion as possible. The key to success is to move as quickly as possible in both directions of the exercise. Do not slow down during any part of the motion. This will teach the nervous system to turn muscles on and off more quickly and help in the development of hand speed.

The 12-exercise Warrior Complex Set is as follows. The exercises must be performed in this order to keep the flow and challenge different muscles at different times. The exercises are 1. Straight-Leg Dead Lift 2. Shrug 3. Clean 4. Press 5. Upright Row 6. Bent-Over Row 7. Snatch 8. Good Morning 9. Triceps Press 10. Biceps Curl 11. Bench series 12. Pullover

When done at maximum intensity, this exercise should get your heart rate close to maximum. We always reach at least 180 beats per minute. Wait until the heart rate is back down to under 120 before beginning the next set. Each week monitor how long the recovery in between sets takes to get your heart rate back to 120. This time should decrease every week as you continue to perform these exercises. Use this exercise with some of your training partners who feel that they are in shape and believe that light weights can't improve performance. When they need to take a break or can't seem to recover, you will show them that training is about survival of the fittest.

START POSITION

Start by standing with the bar held at the hips, with arms extended, as shown.

1. STRAIGHT-LEG DEAD LIFT

While keeping the legs and low back straight, bend forward at the waist, and then return to standing upright.

2. SHRUG

From the start position, pull the shoulders up toward the ears while keeping the elbows extended, and then lower under control.

3. CLEAN

From the start position, quickly jump and shrug the weight up to the clean position, as shown.

Lower the weight back to the start position and repeat.

4. PRESS

From the finished position of the clean, with the bar at shoulder height, press the bar over head by extending at the elbows.

Lower and repeat.

5. UPRIGHT ROW

Begin with a narrow grip on the bar, with the bar hanging at waist height, as shown.

Pull the elbows up to ear height and bring the bar up to the chest.

Lower under control and repeat.

6. BENT-OVER ROW

Begin by leaning forward, with a wider than shoulder-width grip on the bar at knee height, as shown.

Pull the elbows up to shoulder height, so that the bar touches the chest at nipple level.

Lower under control and repeat.

7. SNATCH

Begin in the start position with the bar held at waist height.

Quickly jump and shrug the bar upward so that the bar finishes overhead, as shown.

Lower under control and repeat.

8. GOOD MORNING

With the bar across the shoulders, lean forward at the waist while keeping the low back flat and the knees close to extended.

Return to standing and repeat.

9. TRICEPS PRESS

From the finish position in the snatch, bend at the elbows and lower the bar behind the head, as shown.

Press the bar up by extending at the elbows to the original position.

10. BICEPS CURL

Begin in the start position, only this time with an underhand grip on the bar, as shown.

Curl the bar up to chin height.

Lower the bar under control and repeat.

11. BENCH SERIES

11A. CLOSE-GRIP BENCH

Begin by lying on the back, with a narrow grip on the
   bar, as shown.

Bring the weight to the chest while keeping the elbows
   close to the body.

Press the weight back up by extending at the elbows.

11B. WIDE-GRIP BENCH

Begin by lying on the back, with a wider than shoulder-
   width grip, as shown.

Bring the weight to the chest while keeping the elbows
   close to the body.

Press the weight back up by extending the elbows.

12. PULLOVER

Begin by lying on the back, with the elbows bent and tight to the body, as shown.

Let the weight pass overhead and drop toward the floor.

Pull the bar back to the original position.

Running

1. TREADMILL RUNNING

I utilize the treadmill during most of the hurricanes that we perform in the facility. The treadmill is a great tool for building endurance and caloric expenditure in a controllable, small environment.

2. TRACK ENDURANCE WORK

I also like to go to the track and do interval sprint and jogging work.

A sample workout is running 10 100 m sprints, at about 85% of maximum while walking the 100 m curves for the recovery.

Another form I like is sprinting 12–15 40-yard dashes and walking the recovery.

Note: You must ease into this style of training or shin splints are sure to plague you. Give your body time to get ready for this style of training with a few easy weeks of lighter volume.

3. STADIUM STAIR RUNNING

If you have a nice set of stadium stairs nearby at either the local college or high school, they can be a great tool for your stamina training. I like to create different patterns for us to run on the stadiums to keep my warriors fresh. There are an infinite number of ways to use the stairs. The first step is getting out there and trying them out.

A great way to run the stadiums is to run 4–5 5-minute rounds. You can alternate the pace between running hard up the stairs and jogging the side and downward portions.

4. ROAD WORK

Even though some people may think that road work is archaic, I still believe that there is value to this. Not only does it give the warrior improved endurance and caloric expenditure, it also gets the warrior outside and can help to clear the mind.

I don't recommend much over 30 minutes of running, and make sure that the pitch of the road is not too steep and that you have an adequate pair of shoes for this exercise.

ABOVE: The look of fatigue on Mike Corey demonstrates the incredible demand of MMA on the warrior.

LEFT: Maurice Smith's fourth-round victory over Marco Ruas was a test of skill and will.

Fabio Leopoldo uses all of the muscles of his hips to ferociously attack with the triangle.

thirteen

WARRIOR HIP TRAINING

Just like a boa constrictor, the warrior must be able to latch down on his opponent and squeeze the life out of him. Although it may not be apparent, the muscles of the hips are essential in this ability. The muscles surrounding the hips are some of the biggest and strongest in a warrior's arsenal. This chapter is going to focus on the all-important hip abductors, hip flexors, and hip adductors. These muscles are used to squeeze the legs together, spread them apart, and drive the knee forward at the hip joint. In an MMA match a warrior must use these muscles to help generate force during kicks, knees, and punches and to stabilize the hip when shooting in or defending takedowns. On the ground, however, is when these muscles are used often during a fight, and their use is commonly misunderstood by people watching the event.

Many warriors may not understand why the guard is often a safe and powerful position. Not only is it difficult for a fighter to pass an experienced grappler's guard, but the athlete on top is in danger of submission if he is not careful.

The guard position is centered around the hips. If the hips are free, the guard can be maintained, which leaves the warrior at a safe distance and the opponent vulnerable to submission attack. When the hips are overcome or controlled, the warrior in the guard position has now become vulnerable. In addition to its improving grappling technique, developing powerful hip abductors, hip flexors, and hip adductors is critical for keeping an opponent from passing the guard. By no means am I saying get strong hips and you will have a great guard, but I am saying that stronger hips in addition to a great technical guard will make your game better. This chapter focuses on these often overlooked and undertrained muscles that will allow the warrior to develop a vice-grip guard on an opponent.

HIP EXERCISES

1. BAND GUARD PULL

Begin by lying on the back, with a giant elastic band hooked around the ankles, as shown.

Pull the feet up toward the hips as if assuming the open guard position.

Hold for time, and then slowly let the knees return to the extended position.

2. CABLE KNEE LIFT

Begin by standing with the hands holding a support and the weighted ankle back,
   as shown.

Drive the weighted knee forward and in front of the hip.

Lower the leg under control and repeat.

3. GROIN PLATE SLIDE

Begin by standing with the inside of one foot placed against a weight plate, as shown.

Slide the plate across the floor in front of the body while keeping balance.

Repeat for the required distance or number of repetitions.

4. WRAPPING PLATE SLIDE

Begin by standing with the hands against a wall and the toes of one foot placed on a weight plate, as shown.

Slide the plate from the front around the body to the back.

Bring the plate back and repeat.

Sidewinder (ankle band) Series

The ankle band is a great training tool for the hip abductors. Depending on the type that you have, the resistance may be able to be adjusted. Make sure you are using the strongest tension that you can and still be able to complete the exercises. The next three exercises are performed using this tool.

5. SIDE LUNGE

Begin in a half-squat position, with the shoulder blades pulled back.

Step out to the side with the right foot, leading with the heel.

Bring the left foot back to meet the left.

The left foot should be brought back slowly, under control, and the foot should not drag on the floor.

6. BACK ZIGZAG

Begin in the half-squat position, facing backward to the direction you will be traveling.

Drive the right foot backward at a 45-degree angle to the body.

Bring the left foot to meet the right by sliding the whole body to the right.

The left foot should be brought back slowly, and the foot should not drag on the floor.

7. WOBBLE WALK

Begin in the half-squat position, with the feet pulled apart as much as possible.

Take small steps forward, keeping the feet as far apart as possible.

Repeat for the prescribed distance or the required number of steps.

8. CROSSOVER STEP-UP

This exercise can be performed with either a bar or
  dumbbells.

Begin next to a box with the outside foot resting on its
  top and that knee at 90 degrees.

Without using force from the bottom leg, step up onto
  the box from the side.

Slowly lower back to the ground under control and
  repeat.

9. PHYSIOBALL HIP TWIST

Begin with the knees placed on the ball and the hands placed on the ground, as shown.

Twist the hips while keeping the shoulders square so that the side of one thigh is on the ball.

Return to the original position, and twist to the other side.

Alex Schoenauer clamps down with his hip muscles to maintain the closed guard position.

Aaron Stark drives forward with his hips to flatten out his opponent and attacks.

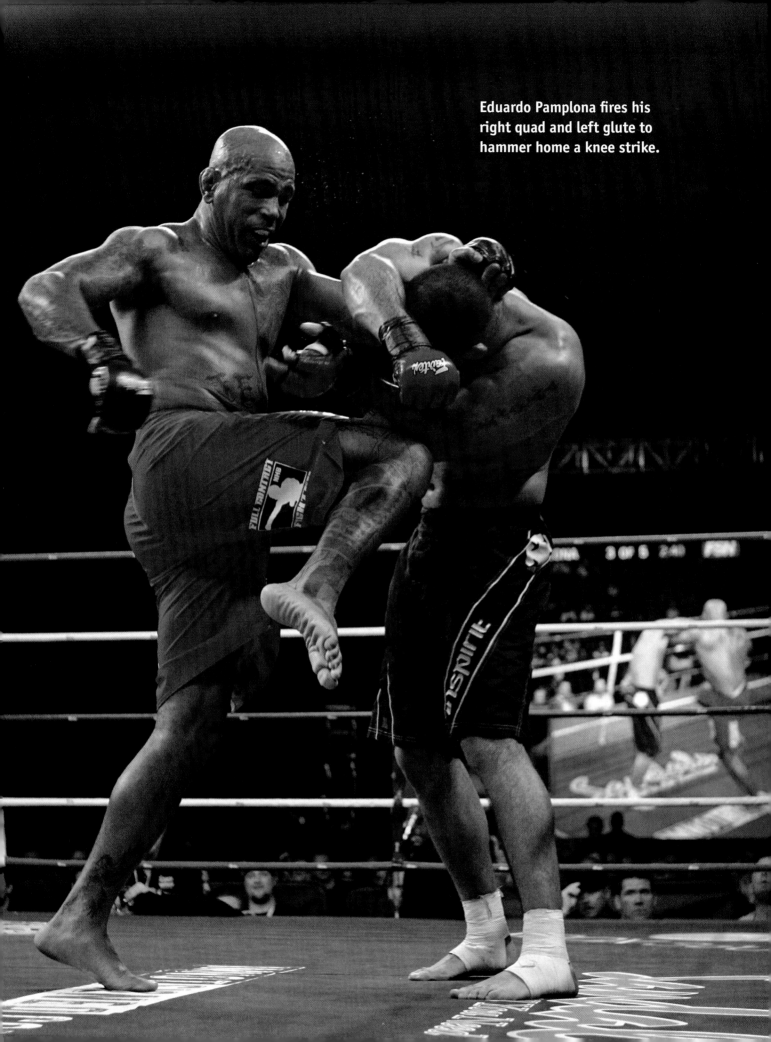

Eduardo Pamplona fires his right quad and left glute to hammer home a knee strike.

fourteen

WARRIOR GLUTES AND QUADS TRAINING

The days of the weak, thin-legged fighter are over. As Bruce Lee once said, "Take power from the ground through your legs, hips, and back." Everything starts from the ground. To properly execute a powerful punch, kick, or takedown, the legs have to be strong. The same goes for powerful sprawls (driving the legs back to prevent a takedown), reversals, and mounts. Without proper leg strength, these are all going to be ineffective in the ring. Today's warrior knows leg training has to take precedence in a warrior's strength work. The gluteal muscles at the back of the hips and the quadriceps in the front of the thigh are some of the largest and most powerful muscles of the warrior's body. Interestingly, these muscles are often atrophied and weak in today's warrior. This is because warriors "mold" their bodies into shapes according to what muscles they use most. When a warrior spends most of his or her training on the ground, that warrior is going to have a classic look: strong forearms, back, and neck but skinny legs with no gluteal and quad muscles to be found. If one looks back at the physiques of many of the fighters of the past, this area is commonly undersized.

Not only must the warrior understand that the hips are an incredibly important area, but he or she must also know that to control an opponent's hips, either on the feet or on the ground during a fight, is to control that opponent. If you are not able to control your opponent's hips during a fight, all of the strength in the world cannot stop your opponent from sprawling away or escaping on the ground and getting back to his feet. Strong hips and the ability to resist a takedown by sprawling and get back to, or stay on, the feet are reasons why many striking fighters, such as Chuck Liddell and Mirko Crocop, are enjoying success today with little use of the ground game during their fights.

The huge glute and quad muscles allow you to explosively sprawl, escape, and are also critical for executing powerful kicks, punches, and lightning-fast takedowns. These muscles are very important links in the powerful chain that connects the muscles all the way from the neck, back, and core down to the feet of a warrior. The thin-legged body type of the past will not work for the warrior of the future. The exercises in this chapter are designed to make legs like oak trees that are lightning fast.

GLUTES AND QUAD EXERCISES

1. SINGLE-LEG BURPEE

Begin by standing tall, and then drop down, with your weight on both hands and one foot.

Hop the weighted leg back to the push-up position.

Return the foot forward, and then stand back up to the original position.

2. PARTNER BODY SQUAT

Begin with the partner across your shoulders, holding under one arm and one leg.
Squat down as far as possible, and return to the original standing position.

3. PARTNER CARRY DRILL

Begin by holding the partner horizontal, under his top leg and bottom shoulder.
The carried partner crosses his ankles and locks his hands around the shoulder of
  the carrier.
Walk for the required distance.

4. PARTNER CROSSOVER DRILL

Begin with the partner across your shoulders, holding under one arm and one leg.

While performing a quarter squat, walk to the side, crossing one foot in front of the other.

Keep the toes pointed forward, and repeat for the required distance on each side.

5. PARTNER SIDE-PUSH LUNGE

Partner #1 stands on the side of partner #2, with the hands on his shoulder.

Partner #1 pushes #2 to the side.

Partner #2 lands in the side-lunge position and has to stop, hold this position, and press back up to standing.

Perform on both sides.

6. PARTNER FRONT-PUSH LUNGE

Partner #1 stands behind Partner #2, with the hands on his shoulder blades.

Partner #1 pushes #2 forward.

Partner #2 lands in the forward-lunge position and has to stop, hold this position, and press back up to standing.

Perform on both legs.

7. PHYSIOBALL WALL SQUAT

Begin in the standing position, with the ball placed behind the back.

Lower into the squat position while leaning into the ball.

Hold the squat position for a 5 count and repeat.

8. TRAP-BAR DEAD LIFT

Begin in the squat position inside the trap bar, as shown.

Stand up by extending the knees, hips, and low back.

Shrug the shoulders at the top of the position.

Lower under control and repeat.

9. BACK SQUAT

Begin with the bar across the shoulders, as shown.

Slowly lower the body under control into the full-squat position.

Press up by extending at the knees, hips, and low back.

10. FRONT SQUAT

Begin with the bar across the front of
  the shoulders, as shown.

Slowly lower the body under control
  into the full squat position.

Press up by extending at the knees,
  hips, and low back.

11. DEAD LIFT

Begin in the squat position, grabbing the bar shoulder-width apart, as shown.

Stand up by extending the knees, hips, and low back.

Lower under control and repeat.

12. WEIGHTED LUNGE WALK

This exercise can be performed with either a bar or dumbbells.

Begin by standing, with the weights in the hands.

Lunge forward with one leg so that the back knee almost touches the ground.

Step forward and press back up to standing and repeat.

13. STEP-UP

This exercise can be performed with either a bar or dumbbells.

Begin with one entire foot resting on a box that elevates the knee at 90 degrees, as shown.

Without using force from the bottom leg, step up onto the box.

Slowly lower back to the ground under control and repeat.

14. EXPLOSIVE STEP-UP

Begin with one foot resting on a box and weighted hands in an opposite arm-and-leg
   relationship, as shown.

Explosively fire the arms as you press forcefully into the box and jump into the air.

After landing on the box, slowly lower the body back to the original position and repeat.

15. PLATE PUSH

Begin on all fours in the push-up position, with the hands on the plate.

Keeping the elbows locked, drive the plate forward, taking strides as big as possible.

Repeat for the required distance.

16. POWER CURL

This exercise has quickly become one of the favorites among our group because it not only builds explosive pulling power but can also add an inch or two to your arms.

Begin by kneeling in front of the bar, with the hands at shoulder-width apart, as shown.
Explode up to the feet while keeping the hips low.
Stand up with the weight as fast as possible, and curl the bar to chin height.
Lower under control, and return to the original position.

17. POWER HIGH PULL

Begin by kneeling in front of the bar, with the hands at shoulder-width apart, as shown.

Explode up to the feet while keeping the hips low.

Stand up with the weight as fast as possible, and pull the bar to chin height.

Lower under control, and return to the original position.

18. ZERCHER SQUAT

Begin in the athletic position in front of a bar placed at navel height.

Clasp the hands together and catch the bar at the folds in the elbow, as shown.

Stand up, holding the bar with the arms, and then lower back to the original position
   under control.

Mike Whitehead drives with his glutes and quads to ram Krzysztof Soszynski into the ropes.

Ryan Schultz uses his right quad and left glute to ferociously attack a game Aaron Riley.

Mike Guymon powers his hips upward with the use of his hamstrings to create distance from Pat Healy.

fifteen

WARRIOR HAMSTRING TRAINING

The warrior must develop the muscles that he cannot see in the mirror. When most warriors are asked to show off "their muscle," most quickly demonstrate the biceps of the upper arm. After reading this book warriors will know that another biceps of the body, the hamstrings, should be the muscle they show off in the future. This area of the body is where warriors must develop some "beef" if they really want to go to the next level. Although this region of the body may not be as popular to work as the upper body, the warrior that addresses this region will surely have the upper hand in battle.

The hamstring group of muscles, which are found behind the thigh, are used in every aspect of MMA. Since this muscle group crosses the hip and the knee joint, there are many important uses that the warrior has for these powerful muscles. During stand-up, the hamstring group helps the warrior to move forward to strike, shoot in, and drive his opponent into the ropes. These muscles also allow dynamic range of motion, decelerate kicks, help to deliver power for punches, and extend the hip when sprawling to defend the takedown. On the ground, these muscles help flex the knee to control an opponent or stop an opponent from passing from guard or half guard and when the warrior has the hooks in while taking the back. These muscles are also used in submissions like the omoplata shoulder lock, the arm bar, and the triangle. Without strength in this region of the body, the warrior is stepping into the ring physically challenged and unprepared for victory.

The exercises in this chapter address motions for both the hip and the knee. Since many motions in MMA—such as the arm bar and triangle submissions, for example—involve both knee and hip strength to complete the movement, there are exercises that address this ability, as well as ones that isolate one joint at a time. An easy way to determine if you need to work this area is to turn to the side in front of a mirror and see if these muscles are flat—if they are, you have a major overhaul ahead. The exercises in this chapter will help you to get the job done.

HAMSTRING EXERCISES

1. PHYSIOBALL HIP POP-UP

Begin by lying on the back, with the heels on the ball and the knees extended, as shown.

Press the heels down into the ball and lift the hips off the ground.

Lower under control and repeat.

2. PHYSIOBALL HAMSTRING CURL

Begin by lying on the back, with the heels on the ball and the knees straight, as shown.

Press the heels down into the ball and lift the hips off the ground while bending the knees.

Lower under control and repeat.

3. SINGLE-LEG PHYSIOBALL HAMSTRING CURL

Begin by lying on the back, with the heels on the ball and the knees straight, as shown.

Press one heel down into the ball and lift the hips off the ground while bending the knee.

Lower under control, and repeat on the opposite leg.

4. HIP POP-UP WITH PLATE

This exercise is one that we have been using for a long time at the school.

Begin by lying on the back, with one heel up on a box or a bench and the other in the air
    with a plate held on the shin of that bent leg, as shown.

Drive the heel into the box and lift the hips as high as possible off the floor.

Lower under control and repeat.

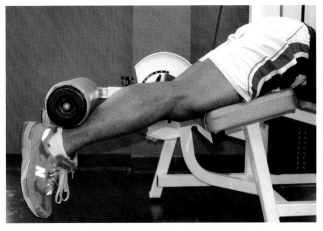

5. HAMSTRING CURL

Begin by lying on the stomach, with the heels hooked under the machine, as shown.

Curl the heels toward the buttocks, and then lower under control for a 5 count.

6. SINGLE-LEG HAMSTRING CURL

Begin by lying on the stomach, with only one heel hooked under the machine, as shown.

Curl the heel toward the buttocks, and then lower under control for a 5 count.

Repeat on the opposite leg.

7. PARTNER HAMSTRING RAISE

Begin on the knees, with the partner holding your feet down at the ankles.

Lower your torso under control to the ground, and return to the starting position.

8. ONE-LEG STIFF-LEGGED DEAD LIFT

This exercise can be performed with either a bar or dumbbells.

Begin by standing on one foot, with the weights in the hands, as shown.

Slowly lower the torso forward at the waist as the free leg rises up behind the body.

From the bottom position, raise the torso back to the original position.

Shad Lierley plants a kick to the chest of Chris Horodecki with the use of his flexible and strong hamstrings.

Ryan McGivern's hamstrings assist in the open guard to keep distance and defend from the attacking Benji Radach.

Both fighters are engaged in a battle that involves the attack of the foot and ankle.

sixteen

WARRIOR FOOT AND ANKLE TRAINING

Without a strong set of feet, the warrior is walking right into trouble. Every fight starts "on the feet." Many fighters during a fight choose to attempt to get "back to the feet" to change the tempo of the fight. During training, the mixed martial artist will practice "feet to floor" drills. With these phrases being so common in the warrior's vocabulary, why then do most warriors never actually train their feet with specific exercises?

The foot is the only part of the body that connects to the ground during stand-up, the clinch, and takedowns during a mixed martial arts fight, in which no shoes are worn. Strength of the feet and ankles is critical, not only to best develop power during strikes and takedowns, but also to lock in the guard and assist in submission attempts on the ground. Understanding this, a warrior must make sure that training is followed to promote foot health and ensure injury prevention. When a warrior's feet are injured, he or she is surely miserable, less mobile, and training is reduced. When training is reduced, the chance for victory decreases.

The exercises in this chapter are designed to promote foot strength, stability, and balance. Since the warrior fights barefoot, much of the training, such as the warm-up and other activities in this book, can be performed barefoot as well. It is often said that the difference between *ordinary* and *extraordinary* is the little *extra*.

FOOT AND ANKLE EXERCISES

1. PARTNER CALF RAISE

Begin with the partner riding piggyback, as shown.

Rise up on the toes as high as possible, and slowly return to the ground.

2. PARTNER DONKEY CALF RAISE

Begin by leaning against a wall, with your partner sitting on your low back, as shown.

Rise up on the toes as high as possible, and slowly return to the ground.

3. CALF RAISE

I have heard top coaches say athletes get enough calf work from running. If this were true, wouldn't these same coaches be against posterior chain work as well? If the hamstrings and glutes and quads are okay to weight-train to improve performance, I am not sure why the calves are being left out. We perform calf raises, have had great success, and it has not led to injury. For an extra effect, toughen up the feet and perform them barefoot.

Begin with the balls of the feet on the edge of the calf raise (with the toes straight or pointed out or pointed in).

Press up onto the ball of the foot as high as possible and hold for 2 seconds.

Lower under control until there is a full stretch on the calf complex.

Perform each toe position for 5 repetitions.

4. TOE-OUT CALF RAISE

5. TOE-IN CALF RAISE

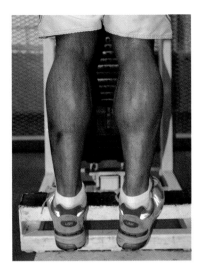

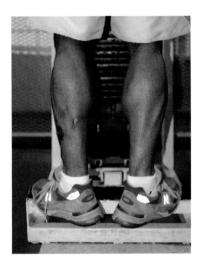

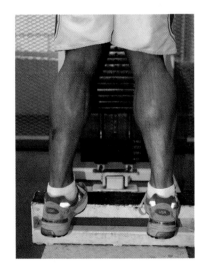

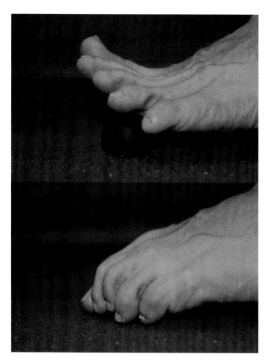

6. BALL SQUEEZE

Just as someone would train their hand grip with a foam ball, I have found the same to be effective for training the foot. I started doing this when I was playing with my cat's toy when I was typing this very book. After a bunch of weeks of training the feet every night, with both high reps and isometric holds, my feet never felt stronger or more useful.

Begin with a small rubber ball under the balls of the feet. Maximally grip the ball with the feet and hold for 5
seconds.
Relax and repeat.

7. PEN FOOT CURL

If you don't have a small ball to squeeze with your feet handy all the time, you can still perform foot curls periodically throughout the day. My game used to be that whenever I was angry at something or someone, I would grip my feet as tightly as possible and put on a big smile. This kept me from getting into trouble and got my feet even stronger.

Another fun way to perform these I learned years ago when I was rehabbing an ankle sprain. It is to pick up a pen with the toes and hold it up for time. Not only is this great for balance, but it will leave your feet burning.

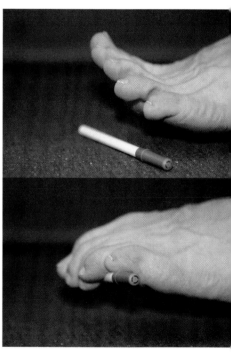

8. TOWEL FOOT CURL

Another great way to build the warrior foot is with towel curls.

Begin with the foot flat on a straightened
towel, as shown.
Curl the toes and pull the towel toward you.
Open the toes and then repeat the curl to
pull more towel.

Ankle Bands

Elastic bands are one of my favorite tools for strengthening the ankle, pre- and postrehab. Using these bands, an athlete can work dorsiflexion, plantarflexion, eversion, and inversion with ease. Depending on the strength of the band, these can be very challenging.

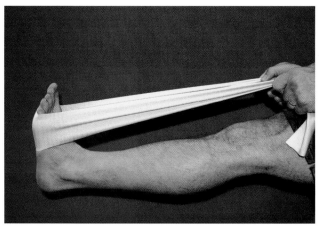 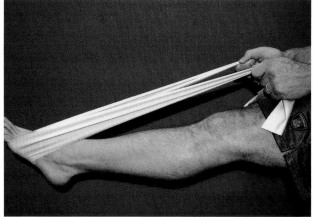

9. PLANTARFLEXION

Begin by sitting, with the band looped around the ball of one foot and the knee straight. Pull to create resistance through the band and push the toe downward as far as possible.

10. DORSIFLEXION

Begin with the feet flat on the floor and the band wrapped around the ball of one foot and held in place, as shown.

Point the toes downward as far as possible, and then pull toes up maximally.

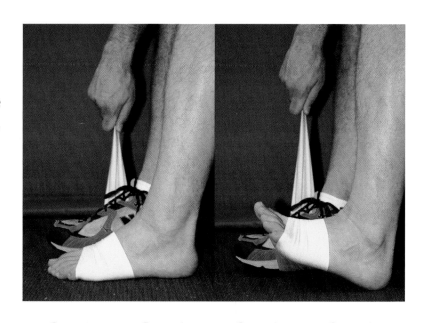

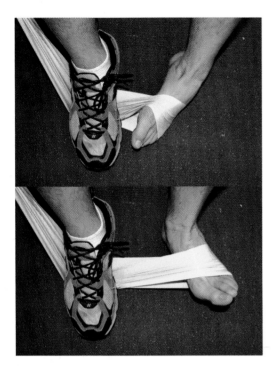

11. EVERSION

Begin with one forefoot wrapped in the band with the other
 foot standing on the band, as shown.
While keeping pressure on the band, evert (point toes up and
 out to the side) the foot as far as possible.
Return under control and repeat.

12. INVERSION

Begin with one leg crossed over another, and the top
 foot wrapped with the band while the other foot
 stands on the band, as shown.
Pull the toes of the top foot toward the ceiling as
 high as possible.
Lower under control and repeat.

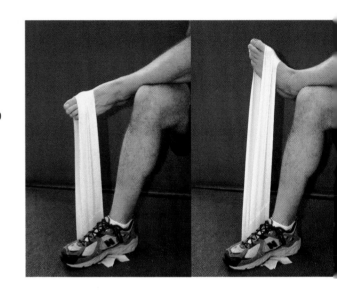

13. BAREFOOT, EYES CLOSED

A final exercise for balance of the foot and ankle that I
like to perform with my warriors is standing on one
foot with the eyes closed. If you try this with your
athletes, especially ones with past foot or ankle
problems, you will be surprised by the results. Since we
rely so heavily on vision for our balance, people rarely
activate and use the internal sensory receptors at the
ankle to balance. With a little practice, people get
better at this, stronger and less injury prone. Once the
warrior masters this exercise, he or she can add a
balance pad, as shown.

Fabio Leopoldo completes the knee bar by anchoring to Ryan McGivern's foot and ankle.

Tap out! Look at the pain induced from a twisting heel hook on the ankle.

Ryan Schultz shows off some amazing flexibility with his head kick to Bart Palaszewski.

seventeen

WARRIOR FLEXIBILITY TRAINING

THE WAY OF LIFE

A man is born gentle and weak.

At his death he is hard and stiff.

Green plants are tender and filled with sap.

At their death they are withered and dry.

Therefore the stiff and unbending is the disciple of death.

The gentle and yielding is the disciple of life.

Thus an army without flexibility never wins a battle.

A tree that is unbending is easily broken.

The soft and weak will overcome.

     —Lao Tzu

The flexible warrior will eventually prevail over the warrior that is strong and stiff. When some warriors think about flexibility, they may imagine some ancient master in a full split on two chairs holding a hundred-pound rock in his hands. Although this is impressive, this may not be the flexibility needed to be successful in MMA. Warriors should imagine flexibility as the fast and precise head kick that rises in an instant from the floor to the opponent's head. The warrior must understand that flexibility is the ability of certain joints of the body to move through a range of motion. When you watch an MMA fight, it is easy to see that every warrior needs to be able to move through certain ranges at many joints of the body. If a warrior lacks flexibility, not only will the warrior be less efficient with his motions and techniques, but there may also be an increased opportunity for injury.

Depending on the style of the athlete (striker, wrestler, grappler), there may be slightly different requirements for flexibility for certain areas of the body. For instance, a grappler may benefit from larger amounts of hip range of motion in order to control the opponent on the ground and to escape from possible submissions. Regardless of the style, however, every warrior should be paying attention to his or her specific flexibility during training.

As seen in the "Warrior Workouts" chapter, every session begins with a warrior warm-up to work on the dynamic range of motion of specific sections of the body. By moving through that warm-up over time, the warrior will increase full-body flexibility. In addition to this dynamic version of stretching, we perform a more static routine following our workouts to relax our body, realign our fibers, and review the session. All 23 exercises in this chapter can be performed after every warrior training session. Each exercise should be repeated 3 times, and each exercise can be held for 5 inhalations and exhalations. This will force the warrior to focus on breathing and calm the athlete after the session. None of the exercises in this chapter should be performed to the point of discomfort or pain. Use only comfortable ranges of motion, and the movements should be performed smoothly in and out of each position.

The warrior must remember that every warrior is different and that each one will attain a different level of flexibility. You may never attain a full split or touch your hands behind your back. That is acceptable, but getting tighter from losing flexibility over time by not working on this area is not. By consistently following the exercises in this chapter, the warrior will develop the suppleness needed to succeed in MMA.

FLEXIBILITY EXERCISES

1. GROIN STRETCH

Begin by sitting, with the soles of the feet touching in front.

Use the elbows to press the knees toward the ground if necessary.

2. V SIT

Begin by sitting, with the knees extended and the feet out to the sides of the body.

Lean forward and attempt to place the hands or elbows forward on the floor.

3. MODIFIED HURDLER STRETCH

Begin with one knee extended and the other folded, as shown.

Lean forward toward the extended leg's foot.

4. SIDE HURDLER STRETCH

Begin with one knee extended and the other folded, as shown.

Lean to the side, with the top hand grabbing the extended leg's foot.

5. KNEE-TO-CHEST STRETCH

Begin by lying on the back, with the hands clasped over one bent knee.

Pull the knee forward as high as possible while keeping the other leg straight.

6. LYING HAMSTRING STRETCH

Begin by lying on the back, with the hands clasped behind the knee or calf of one raised leg.

Pull the leg forward as high as possible while keeping the other leg straight.

7. QUAD STRETCH

Begin sitting with one foot in front of the hip and one behind, as shown.
Lean backward to create more stretch on the quadriceps of the back leg.

8. HIP STRETCH

Begin sitting with one foot in front of the hip and one behind, as shown.
Lean forward to create more stretch in the hips.

9. HIP-FLEXOR STRETCH

Begin in the lunge position, supported on the back knee and the front foot, as shown.
Raise the hand on the same side as the back leg.

10. STANDING CALF STRETCH

Begin by standing, with one foot forward
   and the back foot with the heel on the
   floor.
Slowly lean the weight forward while
   trying to keep the back heel in contact
   with the ground.

11. STANDING HAMSTRING STRETCH

Begin by standing; then reach down to grab the
   ankles while trying to keep the knees straight.
Slowly lower the head and upper body to try to touch
   the face to the knees.

12. LYING GLUTEAL STRETCH

Begin by lying on the back, with one leg crossed over another and clasping the hands
   behind the far leg, as shown.
Slowly pull the hands closer to the chest to create more stretch in the hips.

13. FOOT-BEHIND-THE-HEAD STRETCH

Begin by lying on the back and grab one heel with the opposite side's hand.
Slowly pull that foot up in an attempt to place the foot behind the head.

14. SHOULDER STRETCH

Begin by sitting while holding one arm across the chest at the elbow.
Slowly pull the elbow up and across the chest.

15. LAT AND TRICEPS STRETCH

Begin seated, with one bent arm held overhead by the other arm, as shown.
Use the hand to slowly pull the elbow behind the head to create the stretch.

16. PARTNER PECTORAL STRETCH

Begin seated, with the hands clasped behind the
  head and the elbows held high.
The partner then places his knee against the upper
  back and slowly pulls up and back on the elbows.

17. PARTNER SHOULDER STRETCH

Begin standing, with the partner holding the wrists of the arms extended to the back, as shown.

The partner then slowly raises the wrists without allowing the person to bend too far at the waist.

18. NECK STRETCH

Begin sitting with one hand placed over the head on the opposite side.

Slowly pull the head in an attempt to bring the ear closer to the shoulder.

19. FOREARM STRETCH

Begin seated, with one arm extended at the elbow and the palm facing the floor. Grab the fingers with the opposite hand and slowly pull the fingers back.

20. BICEPS STRETCH

Begin seated, with one arm extended at the elbow and the palm facing the ceiling. Grab the fingers with the opposite hand and slowly pull the fingers down.

21. ABDOMINAL STRETCH

Begin by lying on the back, with the knees bent, feet on the floor, and palms on the floor next to the head.

Press up into the arch position with only the hands and feet touching the floor.

22. LOW-BACK TWIST

Begin seated, with one leg extended and the other leg crossed over it with the knee bent and the foot flat on the floor.

Place the opposite elbow on the raised knee, and slowly twist the torso.

23. SHOULDER ROTATION

Begin seated, with both hands behind the back, as shown.
Slowly attempt to touch the fingertips together.

TOP: Robbie Lawler fires a high kick with the help of some solid dynamic flexibility.

BOTTOM: Ed West uses his flexible hips and legs to attempt to prevent the standing pass by Erik Owings.

Part III

WARRIOR PROGRAMS

Rory Markham gets down to the bare minimum to make weight for the crowd.

eighteen

WARRIOR WEIGHT CUTTING

ave any of you ever watched a weight-class fight in which one warrior looks far bigger and heavier than the other even though they weighed exactly the same amount the day before? Have you ever wondered how a warrior can lose 10–15 pounds in one day for a weigh-in and then gain it all back for the fight with no ill effects? If you answered "yes" to these two questions, then you are ready to learn the art of weight cutting for competition. If you follow the information in this chapter correctly, not only will your risk of complications be decreased, but your performance should go to the next level.

Over my past number of years training mixed martial artists, probably the biggest weakness I found, in terms of knowledge about training, had to do with nutrition. Within this area, there was even less knowledge about body-weight manipulation, or "cutting weight" for a fight or tournament. I categorize cutting weight under nutrition because the two are closely related, but I am not talking now about changing diet. I am talking now about the rapid drop in body weight and rapid weight gain before and after a weigh-in for a competition.

Cutting weight safely takes knowledge, skill, and practice. I have seen warriors have horrendous performances thanks to cutting too much weight, cutting weight too fast, cutting weight too slowly, not rehydrating correctly, and eating incorrectly after their weigh-in. By the end of this chapter, none of these mistakes should ever happen to you.

WHY CUT WEIGHT?

Many people not involved in mixed martial arts do not understand why some-one would subject himself to water and food restriction to cut weight in the first place. I usually explain this with the example of weight classes. Most combative sport competitions have weight limits for certain classes. Since the object of being in a certain weight class is to be the strongest and heaviest person in that class, many warriors cut their weight down to a lower class and then add weight after the weigh-in. In the warrior's mind, he or she is then heavier for the actual fight and has the potential to be stronger than his or her opponent (as long as the opponent doesn't do the exact same thing). The weigh-ins are also usually the day before the fight. This gives the fighters 20–30 hours to reload their bodies following the weight cutting. For anyone that has ever seen Tito Ortiz, Matt Hughes, or Rich Franklin fight, you should understand what I mean. Every time those warriors fight anyone in the same weight class, they always look much bigger and stronger. The Tito Ortiz versus Elvis Sinosic fight, where both fighters weighed in at 204 pounds, comes to mind. At fight time, Tito looked 230 and Elvis looked 180. This should hammer home the fact that if things are done correctly, cutting weight has huge advantages.

DON'T FORGET THE OTHER HALF!

To cut weight, you could stop eating and drinking, or exercise in heavy clothes to sweat a lot, or hop in the sauna for hours. If done correctly, all of these methods will be somewhat effective in cutting weight for a fight or competition. But what about properly putting the weight back on, in a safe and timely manner, to be ready for the fight? That is where people don't have as many answers. If you think you should just eat and drink to feel good, you are going to run into problems. Do not forget that the reconstitution of your body is equally, if not more, important in the cutting-weight-and-gaining-it-back cycle.

Vernon White demonstrates confidence after successfully making weight.

SHEDDING THE PREFIGHT POUNDS

This section covers the techniques for adequate weight loss. Before I begin though, I must remind everyone that their diet should be solid at this point, and you should always be within about 10–12 pounds of the weight you want to reach before the weight cutting begins. Any more than this amount and things start to get very dangerous. This means that you should control your caloric intake long before the fight and get to 10–12 pounds away from the desired weigh-in weight. By doing this, you will have much less to worry about when the fight approaches.

Fluid Restriction

The simplest and most effective way to begin the weight-cutting process is to decrease or stop fluid intake. Your body is constantly losing fluid by breathing, sweating, and urination. Every minute and hour that goes by without you replacing the fluid, you will lose weight. This process takes no extra energy to complete from a fighter, and you can lose up to 5–6 pounds in 24 hours without drinking. My warriors never go over 24 hours without fluid, and we usually start the fluid restriction exactly 24 hours before the weigh-in. Before beginning the fluid restriction, there are some tricks to use to lose the maximum amount of fluid over that 24 hours.

For the fifth, fourth, and third days before the weigh-in, I have my warriors consume 2 gallons of water a day. They carry the gallon jug around with them so they know how much fluid they are taking in. At this time, the warrior can also be more liberal with sodium in his diet (we don't go heavy on the sodium, but a little increase can help later, as you will see). This increased water intake triggers hormones in the body to excrete more urine than usual. This response will be essential in losing fluid the day before the weigh-in. Two days before the weigh-in, the fighter cuts the fluid intake to one gallon of water and cuts out the sodium from the diet. Finally, the last day before the weigh-in, the fighter takes in no fluids, no sodium, and only food that I will describe later. This process is effortless, and requires only a little discipline and tolerance of a dry mouth.

Sweating

The next-most-popular way to decrease weight before a weigh-in is to sweat out fluid from the body. This can be done in a number of ways, and can take off 5–10 pounds of weight in a short period of time, depending on the conditions. This is a great method, because even if the warrior is already lean, there will still be fluid that can be lost. The limitation to this method is that it requires great amounts of energy expenditure and can sap strength from the fight the next day.

The goal when using this method is to take off the weight you need to lose and incur the least possible amount of fatigue doing it.

The simplest way to use this method is to exercise. That can be as simple as running or jumping rope, to as complex as cardio fight circuits involving punching, kicks, takedowns, and sprinting. Depending on how quickly you need to lose the weight and the temperature of the area you are in, you will get a feel for what style you need to use. In addition to the exercise, athletes commonly use plastic suits and heavy clothing to increase the body temperature and enhance the sweating response. Just remember not to overheat. Athletes have actually died from overheating using some of these methods. (I must repeat that the goal is to be within 10 pounds by the day before the weigh-in so that any methods you use don't need to be drastic.)

Delson Heleno and Andre Gusmao running in the 100-degree Las Vegas heat to make the weight.

In addition to exercise, warriors can use a sauna or hot bath or shower to lose fluid as well. A dry sauna is the most powerful of the three for weight loss, and this loss should be monitored. Time spent in the sauna or hot showers should be at small 15–30-minute intervals to check weight loss. This brings up a great point: it would be a good idea to travel with your own scale to monitor how much weight you are losing. The last thing you need to do is lose too much weight.

Delson shows us all that making the weight is no easy task.

Bowel Emptying

Another method to lose weight is to empty the bowels the day before the weigh-in. This is another method that requires no effort and will not hurt performance if done correctly. Your bowels, or stomach and intestines, are up to 28 feet long and contain up to 5–7 pounds of material at all times. The food that has been ingested over the last 24 hours is all still contained in this set of tubes. This material does not help performance and is actually waste. By clearing out the bowels, a warrior can lose another 5 pounds without having to do anything. The secret is in the methods.

Two days before the weigh-in, a warrior will already be eating less if he has to lose critical pounds. The day before the weigh-in, he should not be eating much at all (to be discussed later). That material that is still in the gut from the day before, however, must be cleared. How we choose to do this is with a very gentle, all-natural laxative. There are much more powerful drugs out there that do this, but you should not be using them. They can hurt your performance and leave you feeling horrible. By taking the gentle, natural laxative before you go to bed the night before the weigh-in, you should wake and be able to clear your bowels completely. Remember that you would do this only if you felt you were not going to make the weight using the methods described before this.

Diuretics

I hate to even bring up this method, but I must because in the past I have seen diuretics used incorrectly by fighters trying to cut the last few pounds. There are natural and drug diuretics out there that can help you to lose up to 10 pounds or more in fluids. I must say, if you were at the right starting point and you followed the methods already outlined in this chapter, this should not be an area that you need to worry about. This method is more dangerous than the others, and can lead to electrolyte imbalances and decreased performance. An all-natural, gentle diuretic is dandelion root. If a

Delson eyes the scale during his weight cut.

diuretic is a must, it should be used the day before the weigh-in, so as not to have problems during the fight.

Eating

Yes, I did put eating as something to do while you are cutting weight. You must make sure that your blood-sugar levels are normal during this process, or else you are going to feel horrible and have no energy for the exercise aspect of the weight cutting. The last thing you want to do at this point is take in fluids with sugar or heavy food. That is why we use a simple energy bar to get the job done. The bar weighs only a few ounces, but it will give you some sugar and fuel that your body can use during the fluid-and-food fast.

YOU MADE IT, NOW WHAT TO DO NEXT

Okay, you made the weight and you are feeling good. Now, as soon as you get off the scale, you need to start refilling your body with everything you lost. As I said before, this piece of the process is as important as the weight reduction. Most warriors make big mistakes here that end up leading to disaster during the fight.

When you are cutting weight, your plasma blood volume decreases, and your blood pressure can increase as a result. In addition to this, your resting heart rate can go up, you can experience fatigue, and you can feel psychologically weak. You need to make sure you reverse these processes, not only as quickly as possible, but correctly and completely. Most people ram a bunch of food and water back into the system right after the weigh-in, but they do not finish the job.

After the weigh-in, you should eat small meals at regular 30-minute intervals. It is critical that you make sure you take in carbohydrates at this time to regain the proper blood-sugar levels. Firing a ton of food down immediately after the weigh-in is going to leave you feeling bloated and sick. Your body won't be able to use all the food at once anyway, and it will just sit there. Smaller meals will digest and then clear the stomach, and you will be able to eat again shortly. We actually have our warriors continue to eat all the way up to a few hours before the fight the next day. Eat meals that you are comfortable with. Don't start to do anything different.

Even more important is getting the fluid balance back. You should immediately take in fluids following the weigh-in and continue to drink at regular intervals. The ultimate goal for my fighters is to see a clear urine stream, which is when we know we are back to normal. This can take 1–3 gallons of fluids over the next day to replace the 10 or more pounds that have been lost. Don't rely on the thirst response, because it will not be accurate. You need to keep drinking to make sure that the blood plasma—the fluid space between the cells and the cells themselves—is refilled. An IV is also a good option here, but it should be administered *only* by a skilled medical professional. There are many dangers involved in this procedure. An IV is usually used as a last resort or in a medical emergency. If everything, from the weight cutting to the weight regaining, has been done correctly and you have 24 hours until the fight, there should be no need for intravenous fluids.

A FEW PIECES OF ADVICE

A main motto of mine is, never try something new a week before the fight. This includes new techniques, new foods, new equipment, and especially weight cutting. This is something that needs to be practiced, just as you would ground or stand-up techniques. In a fight you would never attempt a technique that you have never tried before. You must think the same way about cutting weight. You need to understand everything about it. You must know how to do it, how long it will take your body to lose the weight, and exactly how your body is going to feel. If you don't ever practice it, you are going to add stress and potential disaster to your plan. Practice, and the better you master the weight cutting, the easier it will be to perform when the time comes.

At weigh-ins another mistake I have seen is that of fighters who think they made the weight but are still too heavy. This occurs when a fighter weighs himself only on his scale and does not use the official scale for the event. Remember that you will have access to the official scale, and you should monitor your weight according to it. This is the only way to know if you have made the weight or not. The last thing you need to be doing is frantically exercising to try to cut weight in the last few minutes. The less stress and adrenaline release, the better.

Remember that weight cutting is an art and must be taken very seriously. When used correctly, it can be a powerful tool that can lead to victory. When used incorrectly, it can be a powerful obstacle that can lead to defeat or worse. This, like any art, must be practiced a number of times in advance. Only then can a warrior begin to truly understand its power.

Rolles Gracie enjoys a postworkout shake after
another hard day of training.

nineteen

WARRIOR PERFORMANCE NUTRITION

When you chose to be involved with mixed martial arts, you separated yourself from the regular athletes that do not want to go the extra mile with their training. Most athletes thinking about getting into fighting want to be involved in the speed, strength, flexibility, and technical work, believing that that will lead them to improved performance. This belief is true, but do not forget one important piece of training that cannot be left out if you are going to reach your potential. That piece is what we call *performance nutrition*.

You are first and foremost an athlete. This means you cannot feed your body with the same food that regular people use. You are special, and have special nutritional requirements if you are going to perform at your highest level. Your body is a high-performance vehicle, and you need to fuel it as such. You, therefore, need to search out quality nutrition information that will help you to eat correctly for the rest of your life as an athlete.

Performance nutrition is important to an athlete for four major reasons. First, you need the proper fuel to sustain your performance out in the ring or on the mat. Second, the correct fuel will also help you to build quality muscle and prevent injury. Third, eating correctly will minimize body fat levels, which will allow you to be faster and improve your endurance. Fourth, following proper nutrition habits will prevent future health risks, lengthen your career, and lead to increased self-esteem.

This chapter is not designed to be the be-all and end-all for your nutrition. It contains valuable information about how to eat as an athlete. I am not going to get too deep into the science, but I will give you the practical insight that you need to be a successful athlete.

As I often say during training, "You can't put on your tie before you put on your shirt." Before you should worry about whether you even need supplements or not, first begin with the basics. All too often, athletes will jump to the extras, before they have done their groundwork. Nutrition should first be seen as simple before you try to look at it as complex. For all of my fighters, I begin by asking them to start with the following six pieces of advice for their first month of training:

1. Make sure you drink plenty of water throughout the day. (Avoid soda and high-sugar juices.)
2. Eat 5–6 smaller meals throughout the day instead of 2–3 larger ones.
3. Avoid products containing high amounts of sugar, high-fructose corn syrup, and fat.
4. Make sure that there is a balance of protein, carbohydrate, and fat in every meal that you eat throughout the day.
5. Make sure that you have a high-quality postworkout meal immediately following exercise such as a carb-protein shake.
6. Try to eat 1 hour before exercise or a training session.

Although these six guidelines may seem simple to follow, I rarely see athletes that have the discipline to stick to it. Challenge yourself with the following question: "What is more important to me? To be successful in MMA or to eat poorly?" If you answered to be successful in MMA, then your decision has been made. Now you need to stick to it.

Performance nutrition as a concept has five basic areas:

I. BASIC PHYSIOLOGY: THE SIX BUILDING BLOCKS OF LIFE

I feel that physiology is the most important "ology" an athlete can know. I am talking about human physiology, which can be defined as the science of the functions of the human body and the chemical and physical processes involved. The better you understand how the body works, the better able you are going to be to train and feed it.

There are six building blocks of life. Simply put, if you are missing any of these components from your diet, you are going to die. This is stated not to scare you, but to help you remember. These six building blocks are water, carbohydrates, proteins, fats, vitamins, and minerals. A basic understanding of the functions, sources, and appropriate amounts of each of these building blocks is essential for optimal performance. Without this knowledge, there is no basis for how you choose to eat.

Water

The body is 70 percent water. Your muscles are 80 percent water. You can go without food for some time without dying, but only a few days without water.

As an athlete, you are constantly losing water to the environment, and it must be replaced. Most athletes do not do this at the correct rate, and most are, therefore, in a chronic state of mild dehydration. This has a huge effect on performance and injury. Being dehydrated just 2–3 percent can produce adverse affects in performance.

Our simple analogy is, picture a muscle cell of your body as a grape. Then picture a dehydrated muscle cell as a raisin. Now ask yourself which one you would like to use when you are staring at your opponent across the ring.

My Challenge to You: Drink nothing but water for a week, and drink a lot of it. Try to drink an ounce for every pound that you weigh, and see how you feel.

Carbohydrates

Carbohydrates are one of the important energy sources for the body. Carbohydrates are also the most abused food component in America and one of the biggest reasons for obesity, diabetes, and death in this country. Utilizing carbohydrates correctly is critical for the performance of an MMA athlete.

Now, don't let me scare you too much. There are good and bad carbohydrates. The problem is that most people are eating the bad ones. Did you know that the average American eats 145 pounds of sugar per year? This table sugar, or sucrose, has no nutritional value and is fattening up our country and causing today's youth to develop diabetes at an alarming rate.

There are a few things I would like you to know about carbohydrates: there are simple and complex versions, and there are best choices. The difference between simple and complex carbs that you need to know is that the body digests and handles them differently. Simple carbohydrates such as fructose and sucrose are immediately processed by the body, while the complex versions such as starches and fibers take much more time. Great choices of simple carbohydrates would be fruits and vegetables. These are common choices that most people avoid. You must get beyond this and add fruits and vegetables to as many meals as possible. Complex carbohydrates take a longer time to process. Great choices of complex carbohydrates would be oatmeal and potatoes. I know there are a lot of low-carb dieters out there, but the carbs are essential for the athlete. I also know some people shun rice, pasta, and bread, but for the athletes that are still eating them, please make the right choice. Eat the version that has color. What I mean is choose brown rice over white, wheat bread over white, and whole wheat pasta over regular. Just these simple choices can start to help.

A final note about the dangers of hidden carbs that aren't good for you: Just take a look at the ingredient labels on many of the things you regularly eat. If high-fructose corn syrup is a major ingredient you keep seeing over and over, throw that food out. It is no good for you.

Protein

This is the building block that every athlete wants to jump to. This is the component that no athlete seems to be able to get enough of. Protein is the building block of muscle, and it is essential for repair. Protein is something that should be eaten at every meal in some portion, but many athletes focus too strongly on it. Great choices of protein are egg whites, chicken, fish, and lean beef.

Your body can process only so much protein at one time (some sources say around 30–40 grams), and many athletes exceed that at certain meals of the day, without the proper balance of the other building blocks. Don't eat too much at one serving. This is where having more meals throughout the day is going to make sure you are going to take in the protein that you need for the day. This is something that I am going to discuss later.

Fat

Here is the building block that everyone seems to think is the enemy. Yes, it is true if you eat too much fat, you will get fat. What everyone must remember, though, is that fat is essential in our diet for insulation, our cell membranes, our nerve conduction, and it is an important energy source, as well. Just as with all of the other building blocks, without fat, you are going to die.

There are a number of fats out there, and some are essential for performance. Overall, there are three types of fats. Saturated fats can be described as fats that are solid at room temperature. The fats found in a steak or butter are excellent examples of a saturated fat. There are also monounsaturated and polyunsaturated fats. Some of them are good for you, and some of them are cancer just waiting to happen. Numerous oils, such as olive oil, fish oils, canola oil, peanut oil, etc., are examples of good types of fats. Many oils are healthy, and some are good only for lubing up your car. The process of hydrogenation converts fat into a trans-fatty acid. When you look at the heart attack, stroke, and cancer rates jumping through the roof in this country, these trans-fatty acids are a great suspect. Trans-fatty acids go into your cells and change the DNA inside, because the body cannot assimilate the fat. Then the damaged cell replicates. This replication is also called cancer. You might as well just dip your food in a vat of poison. The good news is that soon trans-fatty acid content will be included on the labels of everything that you eat.

The last piece to remember about fat is that it is not just what type you eat, but how much of it you eat. Fats are not always bad, but too much of certain fats is. Try to select the better fats I have mentioned, and keep them to about 30 percent of your diet.

Vitamins and Minerals

Vitamins and minerals are essential for the growth, normal metabolism, and development of the human body. They are regulators of certain metabolic processes of the body, and without them, diseased states will occur.

If you are eating properly, and your food is nutrient dense, adding vitamins and minerals to your diet may not be necessary. Since many athletes, however, do not eat well enough, and much of the food they eat is not nutrient dense, there may be a need for supplementation of certain vitamins and minerals. This will be covered in the supplement section of this chapter.

II. THERMODYNAMICS

If you could be a car, what kind of car would you like to be? Most people say Ferrari or Lamborghini, but neither of them is the fastest, most specialized car for performance that you could be. I would like you to think of a dragster. You know, one of those cars with the giant back tires, the engine that is just pouring out of the front of the machine, and the spoiler that makes sure it keeps this beast from being airborne. That is specialized for speed and power. When you think of that car, you realize that not only does it need fuel, but this fuel must be in the right amounts and have the right components, and it is very different from what other cars need. This is the philosophy behind performance nutrition. You are a specialized athlete that needs the right amounts and components of fuel for optimum performance.

One of the simplest areas to start with when describing how much to eat is thermodynamics. When I describe thermodynamics to our athletes, I first ask them to simply picture a scale in their minds. One side of the scale is for "calories in" and one side is for "calories out." Whichever side at the end of the day is heavier will decide if you gained or lost weight that day. Quite simply, if you take in more than you expend, you will gain weight. If you burn off more than you take in, you will lose weight. Period.

At this point, you should be asking yourself, "Well, then how many calories do I need a day?" If you cannot answer this question, everything else that you do with your diet is really guesswork. You could be eating all the right things, but if you take in too much or too little of it, you may not be getting the results you are after. A simple formula that we like to use to help determine how many calories you need for a nontraining day is 11–14 multiplied times body weight, in pounds. So, if you weigh 200 pounds, your caloric intake should range from 2,200 to 2,800 calories per day. Depending on how active your job is and how intense you work out that day, you can also add more calories. For instance, if you are active at work, add another 30 percent more calories to this number. In addition to this, add the estimated amount of calories burned during training to get the training-day expenditure. Monitor your weight as you go along, and if you are losing or gaining too much weight, alter the calories 100 at a time to find your optimal range for what you are looking to do. This should lead the athlete to the understanding that thermodynamics is about knowing how much fuel to put into the machine every day.

III. SHOPPING FOR FOOD

Just like throwing a great punch or executing a powerful throw, shopping for food takes training. You need to have the right information and, once you do, make the right moves. You may not know this, but right now there are marketing executives out there thinking up ways to get you to poison yourself and limit your career. They are paid big money to do this, too. What do I mean? Well, if you have ever walked down any of the aisles in your supermarket, they have surely gotten you.

The challenge is there for you to resist and instead make the right choices. It all starts with what I call "Shopping the Perimeter." If you look at every supermarket, the meats, fruits, vegetables, and eggs are all on the perimeter of the store. All of the poison is located on the inside of that perimeter. Think about it, the juice aisle, the soda aisle, the cookie aisle, the cereal aisle, the potato chip aisle, the frozen food aisle. You have seen them, and the marketing slogans, colors, and commercials have gotten you. But you need to be strong and resist. You will be armed with one simple slogan for success: If you can't hunt it down, fish it out of the sea, pick it off a tree, or dig it out of the ground, then do not eat it. Stick with this, and you will be making good food choices. You may think this is hard to do, or impossible, but all of that food is waiting for you on the perimeter. Avoid canned, colored, processed, and synthetically made junk at all costs. You body is going to thank you for it with higher energy levels, faster recovery, and improved performance. All of those attributes are critical to success in MMA.

IV. SHOPPING FOR SUPPLEMENTS

One of the most common topics about nutrition that fighters want to understand is supplements. The reason I think this is funny is that most of those athletes who are interested in taking supplements have horrible diets! Remember, don't put on your tie before you put on your shirt. You must first fix you diet and then see what you need to add. Look at the term "supplement" itself. It means something that completes or makes up for. With a proper diet, there are not going to be many things that need to be supplemented, and there are many products out there that just plain don't work. What I am going to cover is what I feel are necessary supplements for the hard-training MMA athlete. However, it is a good idea to check with your health care professional before taking any supplement.

Whenever athletes are asked what is the most important meal of the day, most of them automatically respond, "Breakfast." I feel this is incorrect. The most important meal to us is the postworkout meal. I like this meal to be in liquid form, to be easily digested. After the workout, your body is in catabolism and starving for the carbohydrates and protein that it needs to recover and repair. This meal can start the recovery process quicker and help ensure progress. It should be taken immediately following the end of the workout. When most people think of a shake, they think of a protein shake. Protein is important to us at the postworkout meal, but you cannot forget about the carbohydrates. I like a 4–5 to 1 ratio of carbs to protein in our postworkout shake. So, if the shake contains 20 grams of protein, my athletes will take in 80–100 grams of carbs afterward as well. Simple carbs and whey protein are great choices here. You can buy a premade postworkout shake, or you can even just mix in the right amount of whey protein with a sports drink. In addition to the basic carbs and protein at this time, I recommend a good antioxidant vitamin (for its ability to decrease the effects of free radicals that are produced by intense exercise), and possibly creatine or L-glutamine if you feel that is necessary once you read the descriptions that follow. This meal is critical. You should then eat again in about one hour.

When I ask, "What is the most important meal besides the postworkout meal?" most athletes again answer, "Breakfast." No, not yet. The preworkout meal comes next. What you ingest before the workout has a lot to do with how that workout will go and the catabolism that takes place. I like my athletes to eat 1–2 hours before the workout, and then have a small liquid mix of 30 grams of carbs and 10 grams of protein immediately before the workout.

Now it must be breakfast, right? Well, yes and no. After the post- and preworkout meal, every meal is very important to the specialized MMA athlete, so you want them all to be perfect. You are eating now for performance, so, in fact, there is never a traditional meal that doesn't count as much as another.

There are a few other supplements that I would recommend every MMA athlete pay attention to. The first is a good encapsulated multivitamin. With the amount of stress you are putting your body through, and the poor air and other conditions that surround us every day, I believe a multivitamin is important. Even if you are getting most of what you need in your diet, you can never be too safe. The second supplement I would recommend is creatine. This is the most studied supplement in the history of supplements, and the research is overwhelming in terms of improved performance and recovery. Although there are some "myths" out there of cramping and pulls using this product, I have not seen those claims supported in the literature. I like my athletes taking 10 grams per day on training days and 5 grams on nontraining days, for as long as they are training for upcoming bouts. The third supplement I would like to mention is L-tyrosine. This is an essential amino acid that acts as a mild stimulant during workouts. It is linked to chemicals in the brain like serotonin, and many of my athletes enjoy improved workouts when they take the product prior to training. Experiment for yourself, but my athletes have found around 3,000 mg before the workout improves training. Finally, L-glutamine is another essential amino acid that I recommend to my athletes. This amino acid has been linked to improved recovery and immune response in athletes. I like my athletes taking anywhere from 5 to 10 grams before training and bed on training days.

V. READING LABELS

Another important skill that I think MMA athletes have to have besides punching, wrestling, and submissions is how to read a food label. The government, which may not always steer you in the right direction for what to eat, at least provides you with the ingredients and makeup of the food that you are eating. Reading these labels is essential in order for an athlete to know how many calories he ingests in a day, as well as what the composition of those calories are.

Having stated the importance of reading labels, I will now state that if you are reading a lot of labels, you may not be eating much of the right food. Last time I checked, there was no ingredient label on an apple or a chicken breast. Remember that most of the food you should be eating should follow the "If you can't hunt it, pick it, or dig it up . . ." rule. That being said, and coming back to most people's reality, you are going to eat things with labels on them, so you should know what they mean.

The first misleading thing to pay attention to is what is considered a serving size according to the label. For instance, you may have a big bowl of cereal or drink a 32-ounce sports drink and think you took in only the number of calories listed on the box. If the serving size is 1 cup of cereal or 8 ounces of sports drink, you may have just quadrupled the calories, and everything else listed on the label, without being aware of it.

After you know the serving size (and try to stick close to it), you can look at the total number of calories and find out what portion of those calories are made up of protein, carbs, or fat. The way to figure this out is to multiply the number of grams of protein or carbs in the serving by 4 (calories) and the grams of fat by 9 (calories). Then divide the total number of calories by that number to know the percent of each. This breakdown of what you are eating will show you how balanced your food really is.

The next thing that I think is most important is not the amount of sprayed-on vitamins the product has (take your multi every day to be sure), but the ingredient list. The ingredients are listed in order of the amount of each substance that is in the product, from the most to the least. So, if your cereal's first ingredient is corn and the second listed is high-fructose corn syrup, you can be pretty sure you should throw out the cereal and eat the box; it's healthier for you.

Another important thing to do with the food label is to identify the amount of sugar and sodium that is in your food. Processed foods are packed with sugar and salt. Not only are these two ingredients killers of performance, they are also killers of people. When you start to be aware of how much sugar and salt you are taking in every day, you will then have control.

A final element that I like my athletes to note is the amount of fiber that is in the food they are eating. There are two types of fiber: soluble and insoluble. All too often, many athletes are not getting enough fiber. Being aware of this will help you to get closer on track. Try to get in about 25–30 grams of fiber in your diet per day. Great choices here are dark leafy vegetables and whole grains.

I hope this nutrition section gives you the simple tools you need to take your game to the next level. An important thing to note among all of this information is that your performance is determined not solely by what you eat, but also by when you eat. Make sure to follow the guidelines I have set out for not only the types of food to ingest, but also the timing of those meals.

SAMPLE MENU (WEIGHT LOSS)—2,000 CALORIES

	CHOICE ONE	CHOICE TWO	CHOICE THREE	CHOICE FOUR
Breakfast *300 Calories*	1 Whole-Wheat English Muffin w/ 1 ½ Tbsp Natural Peanut Butter	1 Cup Cooked Plain Oatmeal 1 Tbsp Raisins 1 Tbsp Walnuts	3 Egg Whites 1 Thin Slice Cheese 2 Slices Whole-Wheat Toast	1 ½ Cups Cereal (<6 gm sugar per serving) 1 Cup Skim Milk
Lunch *500 Calories*	Turkey Sandwich (no cheese) on Whole-Wheat Bread, Wrap, *or* Pita (3–4 slices turkey on sandwich) *Optional*—Honey Mustard Light Yogurt (<120 Calories)	5 oz Grilled Chicken on Whole-Wheat Bread, Wrap, *or* Pita Each Sandwich =3–4 Slices Ham *or* Roast Beef *Optional*—Honey Mustard Piece of Fruit	2 Slices Whole-Wheat Bread 2 Tbsp Natural Peanut Butter 1–2 Tbsp Low-Sugar Jelly	6 oz Grilled Chicken over Mixed Green Salad Light Dressing Piece of Fruit
Preworkout *200 Calories*	Banana & 10 Almonds	Shake	Light Yogurt w/ 1 Cup Fresh Berries	Granola Bar
Dinner *800 Calories*	*Chicken* 8 oz Skinless Grilled / Broiled /Baked Chicken 1 Cup Cooked Brown Rice, Wheat Pasta, Noodles, *or* Medium Baked White or Sweet Potato Mixed Green Salad *or* Vegetables	*Beef* 6 oz Lean Steak (Sirloin, London Broil, Filet Mignon) 1 Cup Cooked Brown Rice, Wheat Pasta, Noodles, *or* Medium Baked White or Sweet Potato Mixed Green Salad *or* Vegetables	*Fish* 8 oz Skinless Grilled / Broiled /Baked Fish 1 Cup Cooked Brown Rice, Wheat Pasta, Noodles, *or* Medium Baked White or Sweet Potato Mixed Green Salad *or* Vegetables	*Pasta* 1 ½ Cups Cooked Pasta 1 Cup Tomato Sauce 1 Meatball (3 oz lean ground beef) Mixed Green Salad *or* Vegetables
Snack *200 Calories*	1 Slice Whole-Wheat Bread 1 Tbsp Peanut Butter	1 Cup Cereal 1 Cup Skim Milk	Light Yogurt w/ 3 Tbsp Granola	1 Scoop Whey Protein in 1 Cup Skim Milk

SAMPLE MENU—3,000 CALORIES

	CHOICE ONE	CHOICE TWO	CHOICE THREE	CHOICE FOUR
Breakfast *500 Calories*	1 Whole-Wheat Bagel w/ 2 Tbsp Natural Peanut Butter	2 Cups Cooked Plain Oatmeal 2 Tbsp Walnuts 2 Tbsp Raisins 1 Tbsp Brown Sugar	1 Egg / 3 Egg Whites 1 Thin Slice Cheese 2 Slices Whole-Wheat Toast Banana *or* 10 oz Orange Juice	2 Cups Cereal (<7gm sugar per serving) 1 ½ Cups Skim Milk Banana *or* 10 oz Orange Juice
Lunch *700 Calories*	4–5 Slices of Turkey on Whole-Wheat Bread, Pita, *or* Round Roll 2 Tbsp Light Mayo, Mustard, or Honey Mustard Apple	4 Slices Lean Roast Beef on Whole-Wheat Bread, Pita, *or* Round Roll 2 Tbsp Light Mayo or Mustard 2 Tangerines	4–5 oz Grilled Chicken on Whole-Wheat Bread, Pita, *or* Round Roll 2 Tbsp Light Mayo, Mustard, or Honey Mustard	Mixed Greens w/ 6 oz Grilled Chicken *or* Turkey Whole-Wheat Pita Light Dressing 1 Cup Fresh Berries
Afternoon Snack *400 Calories*	Granola Bar & Banana	Shake	250–300 Calorie Meal Replacement Bar & Piece of Fruit	6–8 oz Low-Fat Yogurt & Granola Bar
Dinner *1,000 Calories*	***Chicken / Fish*** 10 oz Skinless Grilled / Broiled /Baked Chicken *or* Fish 2 Cups Cooked Brown Rice, Wheat Pasta, Noodles, *or* Medium Baked White or Sweet Potato 1 Cup Green Veggies *or* Mixed Green Salad	***Beef*** 7 oz Lean Steak (Sirloin, London Broil, Filet Mignon) 2 Cups Cooked Brown Rice, Wheat Pasta, Noodles, *or* Medium Baked White or Sweet Potato 1 Cup Green Veggies *or* Mixed Green Salad	***Turkey Burger*** 2 Turkey Burgers (4 oz each) on Whole-Wheat Bread Lettuce / Tomato / Ketchup 1 Cup Green Veggies *or* Mixed Green Salad	***Pasta*** 2 ½ Cups Cooked Pasta 1 Cup Tomato Sauce 2 Meatballs (lean ground beef) 2 oz each 1 Cup Veggies *or* Mixed Green Salad
PM Snack *400 Calories*	Shake	2 Slices Whole-Wheat Bread 1 Tbsp Natural Peanut Butter 1 Tbsp Jelly	1 ½ Cups Cereal 1 ½ Cups Skim Milk	Apple 2–3 Tbsp Natural Peanut Butter

SAMPLE MENU (GAIN LEAN BODY MASS)—4,000 CALORIES

	CHOICE ONE	CHOICE TWO	CHOICE THREE	CHOICE FOUR
Breakfast **700 Calories**	1 Whole-Wheat Bagel w/ 3 Tbsp Natural Peanut Butter	2 Cups Cooked Plain Oatmeal 1/2 Cup Walnuts 2 Tbsp Raisins 1 Tbsp Brown Sugar	*High Protein* 2 Eggs / 3 Egg Whites 2 Thin Slices Cheese 1 Whole-Wheat Bagel	2 ½ Cups Cereal (<6 gm sugar per serving) 2 Cups Skim Milk Banana 6 oz Low-FatYogurt
Lunch **(11:00 AM–12:30 PM)** **1,000 Calories**	2 Turkey and Cheese on Whole-Wheat Bread, Wrap, *or* Pita Each Sandwich = 5 Slices Turkey 2 Thin Slices Cheese *Optional*—Light Mayo or Honey Mustard Granola Bar	2 Ham *or* Roast Beef on Whole-Wheat Bread, Wrap, *or* Pita Each Sandwich = 5 Slices Ham *or* Roast Beef *Optional*—Light Mayo or Honey Mustard Banana	2 Peanut Butter & Jelly Sandwiches on Whole-Wheat Bread Each Sandwich = 3 Tbsp Natural 2 Tbsp Low-Sugar Jelly Low- Fat Yogurt	2 Tuna Sandwiches on Whole-Wheat Bread, Wrap, *or* Pita Each Sandwich = 4 oz Tuna w/ 1 Tbsp Light Mayo or just Vinegar 1 ½ Cup Fresh Berries
Preworkout **350 Calories**	Banana & 25 Almonds	Granola Bar & Low-Fat Yogurt	Shake	Shake
Postworkout **(within 30 min)** **450 Calories**	Shake	Shake	Meal-Replacement Bar and Piece of Fruit	1/2 Turkey Sandwich on Whole-Wheat Bread & Banana

4,000 CALORIES (cont.)

	CHOICE ONE	CHOICE TWO	CHOICE THREE	CHOICE FOUR
Dinner (7:00–8:30 PM) 1,000 Calories	**Chicken / Fish** 10 oz Skinless Grilled / Broiled /Baked Chicken 2 Cups Cooked Brown Rice, Wheat Pasta, Noodles, *or* Medium Baked White or Sweet Potato 1 Cup Green Veggies or Mixed Green Salad	**Beef** 7 oz Lean Steak (Sirloin, London Broil, Filet Mignon) 2 Cups Cooked Brown Rice, Wheat Pasta, Noodles, *or* Medium Baked White or Sweet Potato 1 Cup Green Veggies or Mixed Green Salad	**Fish** 10 oz Grilled / Broiled / Baked Fish 2 Cups Cooked Brown Rice, Wheat Pasta, Noodles, *or* Medium Baked White or Sweet Potato 1 Cup Green Veggies *or* Mixed Green Salad	**Pasta** 2 ½ Cups Cooked Pasta 1 Cup Tomato Sauce 2 Meatballs (lean ground beef) 1 Cup Green Veggies *or* Mixed Green Salad
Snack 500 Calories	2 Slices Whole-Wheat Bread 2 Tbsp Peanut Butter 2 Tbsp Jelly	2 ½ Cups Cereal 2 ½ Cups Milk	Shake	Apple w/ 4 Tbsp Natural Peanut Butter

Daniel Gracie ices his eye after a rough battle with Allan Goes.

twenty

WARRIORS AND INJURY

If you are a warrior involved with mixed martial arts, you need to face two facts: you will get injured and you will have to learn to deal with pain. There are no "ifs" about these facts, just "whens." With most warriors the crux of the problem I see is not "if" an injury happens, but how the warrior responds to the injury "when" it happens. What I mean is that it is the reaction to the injury, in terms of rehabilitation and continuity of training after the injury, not the injury itself, that is most important. There are many lessons to be learned from every injury. The results of these lessons and how you deal with an injury can make the difference between being average and being a champion. Every injury has something to teach you that can make you better in the future, and there are strategies for responding to an injury that can be implemented in order to work around that injury and move forward. This chapter is going to focus on these lessons and offer insight into how you can learn from every injury and make sure that one never holds back your progress again.

> It isn't the mountains ahead to climb that wear you out; it's the pebble in your shoe.
>
> **—Muhammad Ali**

All too often, a warrior will suffer an injury and stop training. I don't think that any injury should ever result in this. I have seen mixed martial artists break a finger or toe and be out of training for weeks to months. This "pebble in your shoe" should never keep you from moving ahead on your climb to success. Whether you are able to improve another area of the body, your nutrition, work certain techniques or even just your mind, there is always time to find ways toward improvement.

Most people view an injury as a negative experience, but in every injury are actually lessons that can make you a much better fighter. Injuries teach us not only about the modes of injury and how to prevent them in the future, but also about our own power to face adversity head-on, or the strategy to best go around it. What I mean is that all too often an injury is like a brick wall. Oftentimes a warrior will continue to attempt to ram through the wall instead of taking a side step and walking around it. Only by correctly training around your injuries can you learn the correct lessons, heal up, and pass through the injury as a better fighter.

> I had sustained an injury to my ribs prior to the fight. I wore pads on my chest and even the night of the fight I had to have four injections to get through the pain.
>
> **—Sugar Ray Leonard**

When our team experiences an injury, I am always then looking for what I call an outlet. In the quote above, Sugar Ray found an outlet to be able to continue to train for his fight. Over the years, I have experienced from head to toe almost every conceivable injury combat has to offer: broken teeth, lacerated eyes, concussions, neck sprain, nerve impingement, shoulder subluxations, elbow capsule strain, broken hand bones, torn abdominal muscle, separated pelvis, patellar tendonitis, shin splints, shin-bone bruises, sprained ankles, and broken toes. All of these have occurred and my training was never really slowed down, I just found an outlet around them to continue training. This ability to work around injury is something I have taught in my training with my warriors.

DON'T TELL ME WHAT YOU CAN'T DO, TELL ME WHAT YOU CAN DO!

My most recent experience with finding outlets in training was with Fabio Leopoldo, as he was preparing for his most recent IFL fight. I remember Fabio coming in, dejected, with the MRI that displayed the broken bone in his foot. Since he could not walk well and was wearing a boot, he thought that his training would be very limited and perhaps the fight would be off. Immediately we went to work on his outlets for training. It was then that his thinking changed from finding all the things he could not do to finding all the things that he could do. And, as he found out through hard training, there was an endless supply of things that he could do that not only kept him in top shape, but also allowed him to heal at the same time. When we ran, he biked. When we lifted, he lifted. When we sparred on the feet, he sparred on the ground. And when his fight came, he won!

In addition to the broken foot that Fabio had sustained while training for takedowns, Fabio also suffered a laceration over his left eye that required stitches only weeks before the fight. Fabio again employed the outlet technique and was able to heal the eye and win the fight.

Injuries will happen and you have to learn to find the outlets to work around them, but there also are lessons about the possible prevention of injuries in the future. Although many injuries cannot be prevented, there are some that can. Getting injured during hard training is acceptable, but getting injured because of carelessness or laziness is not. In the simplest sense, practicing proper training, technical work, and nutrition is the easiest way to prevent injuries from happening. By understanding your sport and the training that surrounds it, injuries can and should be kept at a minimum. Injury prevention should be a key element of every training session. For you to make progress, keeping old injuries at bay and new injuries prevented must take precedence in your training.

Reject your sense of injury and the injury itself disappears.
—**Marcus Aurelius**

Everything about being successful in this sport revolves around having the best strategy. When it comes to recovering from an injury, warrriors don't usually have a plan in mind. To combat this, I have developed the following ten-step strategy to make sure every fighter has a plan in place when injury does occur:

THE WARRIOR'S STRATEGY FOR DEALING WITH INJURIES

1. Accept that the injury has occurred, and move forward.
2. Examine how the injury happened, so that it never happens again.
3. Find out all you can about the injury and its rehabilitation.
4. Use every method of rehabilitation you can get your hands on.
5. Be consistent and thorough with your rehab.
6. Find the outlets and determine what training you can do around the injury.
7. Focus on areas that you needed to improve pre-injury (nutrition, mental training, certain body regions, etc.).
8. Don't test the injury while healing and reirritate it.
9. Develop a list of the things that the injury is trying to tell you.
10. Don't forget what you learned from the injury for the future.

Some warriors often return from an injury at a higher level than where they were pre-injury, thanks to the lessons that the particular injury had to teach them. Many mixed martial artists do not. I believe that how you view and respond to the injury at hand has a lot to do with that. I view every setback as my opportunity for a comeback. You can view an injury as a problem or a challenge. A problem is something you have; a challenge is something you have . . . to take on. I have been told that this kind of adversity causes some fighters to break and others to break through to new levels. The next time you have an injury, and there will be a next time, take the challenge, go around the brick wall, and pass it to become a better warrior.

A fighter's level of damage is assessed in between rounds.

Delson Heleno
and his NY Pitbull
teammates rip
through a ladder
session.

twenty-one

WARRIOR WORKOUTS

The Training for Warriors System is based on 4 training sessions per week. These training sessions do not include essential mixed martial arts training such as boxing, wrestling, and grappling that a warrior will also need to partake in to be successful in the sport.

The 4 Training for Warriors sessions are 1 upper-body session, 1 lower-body session, and 2 hurricane sessions. During the training week, I recommend that 4–5 days be spent training and that 2–3 days be spent completely recovering. Remember that you get better not from the actual training, but from the recovery after the training. Make sure that recovery is the first aspect of training built into your program.

Since the mixed martial artist must train in all disciplines and get the proper recovery during the week, the warrior must train multiple times per day on training days. I recommend that when multiple sessions are going to occur in your training, make sure that they are 4–5 hours apart. An AM/PM schedule works nicely, if possible.

Beginning on the next page is a sample training week for a mixed martial artist. Depending on whether technical skill or physical fitness is the limitation in your game, more time can be allotted.

8-Week Warrior Workout Plan
Week 1

MONDAY: UPPER BODY

1. **Upper-Body Warm-up 15 min.**
   All 6 Crawls (pgs 59–62) 2 sets of 10 yards each
   All 8 Med-Ball Drills (pgs 63–67) 1 set of 15 throws (10 to each side when appropriate)

2. **Upper-Body Training**
   Neck
   Neck Warm-up (pg 71) 20 reps of Lying Flexion and Extension
   Front Neck Bridge (pg 77) 3 sets for 20 sec.
   Back Neck Bridge (pg 76) 3 sets for 20 sec.
   Chest
   Close-Grip Bench Press (pg 92) 4 sets of 8 reps
   Back
   Chin-ups (pg 121) 4 sets of 8 reps
   Arm and Hand
   Plate Fingertip Pick-up (pg 105) 5 sets of 20 sec. hold
   Plate Pinch Drill (pg 106) 5 sets of 20 sec. hold

3. **Core Training**
   Med-Ball Toe Touch (pg 138) 3 sets of 10 reps
   Med-Ball Triangle Crunch (pg 139) 3 sets of 8 reps on each leg
   Med-Ball Explosive Sit-up (pg 140) 3 sets of 10 reps

4. **Flexibility Training**
   Stretches 14–23 (Chapter 17) 1 rep of 5 inhalations/exhalations each

TUESDAY: HURRICANE

1. **Warrior Warm-up 25 min.**
   All Stationary Warm-up Drills (pgs 43–48) 2 sets of 10 reps
   All Movement Warm-up Drills (pgs 48–50) 2 sets of 20 yards
   All Muscle Activation Exercises (pgs 51–58) 1 set of 8 reps (on each side if necessary)

2. **Heart and Lung: Ladder Session**
   All 8 Ladder Exercises (pgs 174–177) in succession
   for 2 times each through the ladder continuously. Rest after the first set for 2 min. and repeat one more set.

3. **Hurricane Category 1**
   Treadmill at 9 mph and 10% grade for 8 sets of 15 sec., with adequate recovery for heart rate to reach 120 BPM.

4. **Flexibility Training**
   Stretches 1–13 (Chapter 17) 1 rep of 5 inhalations/exhalations each

THURSDAY: HURRICANE

1. **Warm-up 25 min.**

   All Stationary Warm-up Drills (pgs 43–48)
   2 sets of 10 reps

   All Movement Warm-up Drills (pgs 48–50)
   2 sets of 20 yards

   All Muscle Activation Exercises (pgs 51–58)
   1 set of 8 reps (on each side if necessary)

2. **Heart and Lung: Hammer Session**

   Overhead Hammer Strike (pg 171) 3 sets of 8
   reps on each side

3. **Hurricane Category 1**

   Treadmill at 10 mph and 10% grade for 9 sets
   of 15 sec., with adequate recovery to reach
   120 BPM.

4. **Flexibility Training**

   Stretches 1–13 (Chapter 17) 1 rep of 5
   inhalations/exhalations each

FRIDAY: LOWER BODY

1. **Warm-up 10 min.**

   All Stationary Warm-up Drills (pgs 43–48)
   3 sets of 10 reps

2. **Lower-Body Training**

   Hips

   Groin Plate Slide (pg 198) 3 sets of 15 on each
   leg

   Side Lunge (ankle band) (pg 199) 3 sets of 10
   yards on each side

   Glutes and Quads

   Trap-Bar Dead Lift (pg 209) 4 sets of 8 reps

   Hamstrings

   One-Leg Stiff-Legged Dead Lift (pg 222) 2 sets
   of 5 reps on each leg

   Feet

   Calf Raises (pgs 226–227) 2 sets of 10 reps

3. **Core Training**

   Prone Abdominal Plank (pg 144) 3 sets of
   20 sec. holds

   Side Stability Hold (pg 143) 3 sets of 20 sec.
   holds

   Med-Ball Figure 8 Drill (pg 141) 3 sets of 8
   reps on each leg

4. **Flexibility Training**

   Stretches 1–13 (Chapter 17) 1 rep of 5
   inhalations/exhalations each

Martin leads a group of warriors through the warrior workout at his facility.

Week 2

MONDAY: UPPER BODY

1. **Upper Body Warm-up 15 min.**
   All 6 Crawls (pgs 59–62) 2 sets of 10 yards each
   All 8 Med-Ball Drills (pgs 63–67) 1 set of 15 throws (10 to each side when appropriate)

2. **Upper-Body Training**
   Neck
   Neck Warm-up (pg 71) 20 reps of Lying Flexion and Extension
   Front Neck Bridge (pg 77) 4 sets for 20 sec.
   Back Neck Bridge (pg 76) 4 sets for 20 sec.
   Chest
   Close-Grip Bench Press (pg 92) 4 sets of 8 reps
   Back
   Narrow Grip Pull-up (pg 122) 4 sets of 8 reps
   Arm and Hand
   Plate Fingertip Pick-up (pg 105) 5 sets of 20 sec. hold
   Plate Pinch Drill (pg 106) 5 sets of 20 sec. hold

3. **Core Training**
   Med-Ball Single-Leg Kick (pg 139) 3 sets of 8 reps on each leg
   Physioball Knee Tuck (pg 142) 3 sets of 10 reps
   Kneeling Forward Bar Roll (pg 154) 3 sets of 10 reps

4. **Flexibility Training**
   Stretches 14–23 (Chapter 17) 1 rep of 5 inhalations/exhalations each

TUESDAY: HURRICANE

1. **Warm-up 25 min.**
   All Stationary Warm-up Drills (pgs 43–48) 2 sets of 10 reps
   All Movement Warm-up Drills (pgs 48–50) 2 sets of 20 yards
   All Muscle Activation Exercises (pgs 51–58) 1 set of 8 reps (on each side if necessary)

2. **Heart and Lung: Ladder Session**
   All 8 Ladder Exercises (pg 174–177) in succession for 2 times each through the ladder continuously. Rest after the first set for 2 min. and repeat one more set.

3. **Hurricane Category 2**
   Treadmill at 9 mph and 10% grade for 20 sec. for 3 sets with Med-Ball Toe Touch (pg 138) 10 reps and Med-Ball Pike-up (pg 138) 8 reps after each sprint.
   Treadmill at 10 mph and 10% grade for 20 sec. for 3 sets with Boxer's Dumbbell Speed Twist (pg 154) 50 reps after each sprint.
   Treadmill at 11 mph and 10% grade for 20 sec. for 3 sets with Med-Ball Triangle Crunch (pg 139) 12 reps on each leg after each sprint.

4. **Flexibility Training**
   Stretches 1–13 (Chapter 17) 1 rep of 5 inhalations/exhalations each

THURSDAY: HURRICANE

1. **Warm-up 25 min.**

2. **Heart and Lung: Hammer Session**
   Overhead Hammer Strike (pg 171) 3 sets of
   8 reps on each side
   Diagonal Hammer Strike (pg 172) 2 sets of
   8 reps on each side

3. **Hurricane Category 1**
   Treadmill at 10 mph and 10% grade for 10 sets
   of 20 sec. with adequate recovery for heart
   rate to reach 120 BPM.

4. **Flexibility Training**
   Stretches 1–13 (Chapter 17) 1 rep of 5
   inhalations/exhalations each

FRIDAY: LOWER BODY

1. **Warm-up 10 min.**
   All Stationary Warm-up Drills (pgs 43–48)
   3 sets of 10 reps

2. **Lower-Body Training**
   Hips
   Groin Plate Slide (pg 198) 3 sets of 15 on each
   leg
   Side Lunge (ankle band) (pg 199) 3 sets of 10
   yards on each side
   Glutes and Quads
   Trap-Bar Dead Lift (pg 209) 4 sets of 8 reps
   Hamstrings
   One-Leg Stiff-Legged Dead Lift (pg 222) 2 sets
   of 5 reps on each leg
   Feet
   Calf Raises (pgs 226–227) 2 sets of 10 reps

3. **Core Training**
   Prone Abdominal Plank (pg 144) 3 sets of
   20 sec. holds
   Side Stability Hold (pg 143) 3 sets of 20 sec.
   holds
   Med-Ball Figure 8 Drill (pg 141) 3 sets of 8
   reps on each leg

4. **Flexibility Training**
   Stretches 1–13 (Chapter 17) 1 rep of 5
   inhalations/exhalations each

Week 3

MONDAY: UPPER BODY

1. **Upper Body Warm-up 15 min.**
    All 6 Crawls (pgs 59–62) 2 sets of 10 yards each
    All 8 Med-Ball Drills (pgs 63–67) 1 set of 15 throws (10 to each side when appropriate)

2. **Upper-Body Training**
    Neck
    Neck Warm-up (pg 71) 20 reps of Lying Flexion and Extension
    Front Neck Bridge (pg 77) 4 sets for 20 sec.
    Back Neck Bridge (pg 76) 4 sets for 20 sec.
    Band Neck Training (pg 75) 3 sets of 5 reps
    Chest
    Close-Grip Bench Press (pg 92) 4 sets of 8 reps
    Back
    Wide-Grip Pull-up (pg 123) 4 sets of 8 reps
    Incline Dumbbell Clean (pg 76) 2 sets of 10 reps
    Arm and Hand
    Plate Fingertip Pick-up (pg 105) 5 sets of 20 sec. hold
    Plate Pinch Drill (pg 106) 5 sets of 20 sec. hold

3. **Core Training**
    Med-Ball Toe Touch (pg 138) 2 sets of 10 reps
    Med-Ball Triangle Crunch (pg 139) 2 sets of 8 reps on each leg
    Physioball Knee Tuck (pg 142) 2 sets of 10 reps
    Olympic-Bar Twist (pg 148) 2 sets of 8 reps on each side

4. **Flexibility Training**
    Stretches 14–23 (Chapter 17) 1 rep of 5 inhalations/exhalations each

TUESDAY: HURRICANE

1. **Warm-up 25 min.**
    All Stationary Warm-up Drills (pgs 43–48) 2 sets of 10 reps
    All Movement Warm-up Drills (pgs 48–50) 2 sets of 20 yards
    All Muscle Activation Exercises (pgs 51–58) 1 set of 8 reps (on each side if necessary)

2. **Heart and Lung: Ladder Session**
    All 8 Ladder Exercises (pgs 174–177) in succession for 2 times each through the ladder continuously. Rest after the first set for 2 min. and repeat 2 more sets.

3. **Hurricane Category 2**
    Treadmill at 9 mph and 10% grade for 20 sec. for 3 sets with Judo Push-up (pg 85) 10 reps and Med-Ball One-Hand Push-up (pg 88) 8 each arm after each sprint.
    Treadmill at 10 mph and 10% grade for 20 sec. for 3 sets with Physioball Push-up, Hands on Ball (pg 89) 10 reps and Physioball Hip Twist (pg 200) 10 reps after each sprint.
    Treadmill at 11 mph and 10% grade for 20 sec. for 3 sets with Physioball Pike Press (pg 91) 10 reps after each sprint.

4. **Flexibility Training**
    Stretches 1–13 (Chapter 17) 1 rep of 5 inhalations/exhalations each

THURSDAY: HURRICANE

1. **Warm-up 25 min.**

   All Stationary Warm-up Drills (pgs 43–48)
      2 sets of 10 reps

   All Movement Warm-up Drills (pgs 48–50)
      2 sets of 20 yards

   All Muscle Activation Exercises (pgs 51–58)
      1 set of 8 reps (on each side if necessary)

2. **Heart and Lung: Hammer Session**

   Overhead Hammer Strike (pg 171) 3 sets of 8
      reps on each side

   Side Hammer Strike (pg 172) 3 sets of 8 reps
      on each side

3. **Hurricane Category 2**

   Treadmill at 9 mph and 10% grade for 20 sec.
      for 3 sets with Med-Ball Toe Touch (pg 138)
      10 reps and Med-Ball Pike-up (pg 138)
      8 reps after each sprint.

   Treadmill at 10 mph and 10% grade for 20 sec.
      for 3 sets with Boxer's Dumbbell Speed Twist
      (pg 154) 50 reps after each sprint.

   Treadmill at 11 mph and 10% grade for 20 sec.
      for 3 sets with Med-Ball Triangle Crunch (pg
      139) 12 reps on each leg after each sprint.

4. **Flexibility Training**

   Stretches 1–13 (Chapter 17) 1 rep of 5
      inhalations/exhalations each

FRIDAY: LOWER BODY

1. **Warm-up 10 min.**

   All Stationary Warm-up Drills (pgs 43–48)
      3 sets of 10 reps

2. **Lower-Body Training**

   Hips

   Groin Plate Slide (pg 198) 3 sets of 15 on each
      leg

   Side Lunge (ankle band) (pg 199) 3 sets of 10
      yards on each side

   Back Zigzag (ankle band) (pg 199) 2 sets of 10
      yards on each side

   Glutes and Quads

   Trap-Bar Dead Lift (pg 209) 4 sets of 8 reps

   Hamstrings

   One-Leg Stiff-Legged Dead Lift (pg 222) 3 sets
      of 5 reps on each leg

   Feet

   Calf Raises (pgs 226–227) 3 sets of 10 reps

3. **Core Training**

   Prone Abdominal Plank (pg 144) 3 sets of
      20 sec. holds

   Side Stability Hold (pg 143) 3 sets of 20 sec.
      holds

   Med-Ball Figure 8 Drill (pg 141) 3 sets of 8
      reps on each leg

4. **Flexibility Training**

   Stretches 1–13 (Chapter 17) 1 rep of 5
      inhalations/exhalations each

Week 4

MONDAY: UPPER BODY

1. **Upper Body Warm-up 15 min.**
   All 6 Crawls (pgs 59–62) 2 sets of 10 yards each
   All 8 Med-Ball Drills (pgs 63–67) 1 set of 15 throws (10 to each side when appropriate)

2. **Upper-Body Training**
   Neck
   Forward Ball Lean (pg 73) 3 sets of 20 sec.
   Side Ball Lean (pg 74) 3 sets of 20 sec. on each side
   Band Neck Training (pg 75) 3 sets of 5 reps
   Chest
   Close-Grip Bench Press (pg 92) 5 sets of 6 reps
   Back
   Alternate-Grip Pull-up (pg 121) 4 sets of 8 reps
   Incline Dumbbell Clean (pg 76) 3 sets of 10 reps
   Arm and Hand
   Plate Fingertip Pick-up (pg 105) 5 sets of 20 sec. hold
   Plate Pinch Drill (pg 106) 5 sets of 20 sec. hold

3. **Core Training**
   Med-Ball Toe Touch (pg 138) 2 sets of 10 reps
   Med-Ball Triangle Crunch (pg 139) 2 sets of 8 reps on each leg
   Olympic-Bar Twist (pg 148) 2 sets of 8 reps on each side
   Cable and Physioball Side Twist (pg 150) 2 sets of 8 reps on each side

4. **Flexibility Training**
   Stretches 14–23 (Chapter 17) 1 rep of 5 inhalations/exhalations each

TUESDAY: HURRICANE

1. **Warm-up 25 min.**
   All Stationary Warm-up Drills (pg 43–48) 2 sets of 10 reps
   All Movement Warm-up Drills (pg 48–50) 2 sets of 20 yards
   All Muscle Activation Exercises (pgs 51–58) 1 set of 8 reps (on each side if necessary)

2. **Heart and Lung: Ladder Session**
   All 8 Ladder Exercises (pgs 174–177) in succession for 2 times each through the ladder continuously. Rest after the first set for 2 min. and repeat 2 more sets.

3. **Hurricane Category 3**
   Treadmill at 10 mph and 10% grade for 25 sec. for 3 sets with Band Curl (pg 110) 10 reps and Band Pushdown (pg 111) 10 reps after each sprint.
   Treadmill at 11 mph and 10% grade for 20 sec. for 3 sets with Front Plate Raise (pg 98) 10 reps and Plate Truck Driver (pg 98) 10 reps after each sprint.
   Treadmill at 12 mph and 10% grade for 20 sec. for 3 sets with Around-the-Head Plate Drill (pg 99) 10 reps on each leg after each sprint.

4. **Flexibility Training**
   Stretches 1–13 (Chapter 17) 1 rep of 5 inhalations/exhalations each

Success through Sacrifice.

Martin pushes Fabio Leopoldo through another session of hurricane training.

THURSDAY: HURRICANE

1. Warm-up 25 min.

All Stationary Warm-up Drills (pgs 43–48)
2 sets of 10 reps

All Movement Warm-up Drills (pg 48–50)
2 sets of 20 yards

All Muscle Activation Exercises (pgs 51–58)
1 set of 8 reps (on each side if necessary)

2. Heart and Lung: Hammer Session

Overhead Hammer Strike (pg 171) 3 sets of 8
reps on each side

Side Hammer Strike (pg 172) 2 sets of 8 reps
on each side

Diagonal Hammer Strike (pg 172) 2 sets of 8
reps on each side

3. Hurricane Category 2

Treadmill at 10 mph and 10% grade for 25 sec.
for 3 sets with Judo Push-up (pg 85) 10 reps
and Med-Ball One-Hand Push-up (pg 88) 8
each arm after each sprint.

Treadmill at 11 mph and 10% grade for 20 sec
for 3 sets with Physioball Push-up, Hands on
Ball, (pg 89) 10 reps and Physioball Hip
Twist (pg 200) 10 reps after each sprint.

Treadmill at 12 mph and 10% grade for 20 sec.
for 3 sets with Physioball Pike Press (pg 91)
10 reps after each sprint.

4. Flexibility Training

Stretches 1–13 (Chapter 17) 1 rep of 5
inhalations/exhalations each

FRIDAY: LOWER BODY

1. Warm-up 10 min.

All Stationary Warm-up Drills (pgs 43–48)
3 sets of 10 reps

2. Lower-Body Training

Hips

Cable Knee Lift (pg 197) 2 sets of 8 on each leg

Side Lunge (ankle band) (pg 199) 3 sets of 10
yards on each side

Back Zigzag (ankle band) (pg 199) 2 sets of 10
yards on each side

Glutes and Quads

Trap-Bar Dead Lift (pg 209) 4 sets of 8 reps

Hamstrings

One-Leg Stiff-Legged Dead Lift (pg 222) 3 sets
of 5 reps on each leg

Feet

Calf Raises (pgs 226–227) 3 sets of 10 reps

3. Core Training

Prone Abdominal Plank (pg 144) 3 sets of
20 sec. holds

Side Stability Hold (pg 143) 3 sets of 20 sec.
holds

Med-Ball Figure 8 Drill (pg 141) 3 sets of 8
reps on each leg

4. Flexibility Training

Stretches 1–13 (Chapter 17) 1 rep of 5
inhalations/exhalations each

Week 5

MONDAY: UPPER BODY

1. **Upper Body Warm-up 15 min.**
   All 6 Crawls (pgs 59–62) 2 sets of 10 yards each
   All 8 Med-Ball Drills (pgs 63–67) 1 set of 15 throws (10 to each side when appropriate)

2. **Upper-Body Training**
   Neck
   Forward Ball Lean (pg 73) 3 sets of 20 sec.
   Side Ball Lean (pg 74) 3 sets of 20 sec. on each side
   Band Neck Training (pg 75) 3 sets of 5 reps
   Chest
   Weighted Dip (pg 93) 3 sets of 8 reps
   Floor Press (pg 95) 3 sets of 6 reps
   Back
   Wrist/Forearm-Grip Chin-ups (pg 122) 4 sets of 8 reps
   Arm and Hand
   Fat Bar Hold (pg 110) 3 sets of 1 min.

3. **Core Training**
   Olympic-Bar Twist (pg 148) 2 sets of 8 reps on each side
   Olympic-Bar Bus Driver (pg 148) 2 sets of 8 reps on each side
   Cable and Physioball Side Twist (pg 150) 2 sets of 8 reps on each side
   Cable and Physioball Downward Twist (pg 150) 2 sets of 8 reps on each side

4. **Flexibility Training**
   Stretches 14–23 (Chapter 17) 1 rep of 5 inhalations/exhalations each

TUESDAY: HURRICANE

1. **Warm-up 25 min.**
   All Stationary Warm-up Drills (pg 43–48) 3 sets of 10 reps
   All Movement Warm-up Drills (pg 48–50) 2 sets of 20 yards
   All Muscle Activation Exercises (pgs 51–58) 1 set of 8 reps (on each side if necessary)

2. **Heart and Lung: Ladder Session**
   All 8 Ladder Exercises (pgs 174–177) in succession for 2 times each through the ladder continuously. Rest after the first set for 2 min. and repeat 2 more sets.

3. **Hurricane Category 3**
   Treadmill at 10 mph and 10% grade for 25 sec. for 3 sets with Reverse Cable Fly (pg 130) 10 reps and Gi Row (pg 111) 10 reps after each sprint.
   Treadmill at 11 mph and 10% grade for 20 sec. for 3 sets with Knee-on-Chest Bent-Over Row (pg 80) 8 reps on each arm after each sprint.
   Treadmill at 12 mph and 10% grade for 20 sec. for 3 sets with Incline Dumbbell Clean (pg 76) 10 reps after each sprint.

4. **Flexibility Training**
   Stretches 1–13 (Chapter 17) 1 rep of 5 inhalations/exhalations each

THURSDAY: HURRICANE

1. **Warm-up 25 min.**

   All Stationary Warm-up Drills (pgs 43–48)
   3 sets of 10 reps

   All Movement Warm-up Drills (pg 48–50)
   2 sets of 20 yards

   All Muscle Activation Exercises (pgs 51–58)
   1 set of 8 reps (on each side if necessary)

2. **Heart and Lung: Bar Complex Session**

   2 Total Bar Complexes (pgs 184–190) of the 12
   exercises for 6 reps each, finishing each
   complex in under 1 min. 30 sec.

3. **Hurricane Category 3**

   Treadmill at 10 mph and 10% grade for 25 sec.
   for 3 sets with Band Curl (pg 110) 10 reps
   and Band Pushdown (pg 111) 10 reps after
   each sprint.

   Treadmill at 11 mph and 10% grade for 20 sec.
   for 3 sets with Front Plate Raise (pg 98) 10
   reps and Plate Truck Driver (pg 98) 10 reps
   after each sprint.

   Treadmill at 12 mph and 10% grade for 20 sec.
   for 3 sets with Around-the-Head Plate Drill
   (pg 99) 10 reps on each leg after each sprint.

4. **Flexibility Training**

   Stretches 1–13 (Chapter 17) 1 rep of 5
   inhalations/exhalations each

FRIDAY: LOWER BODY

1. **Warm-up 10 min.**

   All Stationary Warm-up Drills (pgs 43–48)
   3 sets of 10 reps

2. **Heart and Lung: Plyo Box Jumps**

   High-Box Forward Jump (pg 178) 5 reps for 2
   sets

   Single-Leg High-Box Forward Jump (pg 178) 5
   reps on each leg for 2 sets

   Twisting High-Box Jump (pg 179) 5 reps on
   each side

3. **Lower-Body Training**

   Hips

   Cable Knee Lift (pg 197) 2 sets of 8 reps on
   each leg

   Band Guard Pull (pg 197) 2 sets of 10 reps

   Wobble Walk (ankle band) (pg 200) 2 sets of 30
   yards

   Glutes and Quads

   Step-up (pg 211) 4 sets of 5 reps on each leg

   Hamstrings

   Single-Leg Hamstring Curl (pg 221) 3 sets of 5
   reps on each leg

   Feet

   Toe-out Calf Raise (pg 227) 3 sets of 10 reps

4. **Core Training**

   Single-Leg Prone Abdominal Plank (pg 144) 3
   sets of 15 sec. holds on each leg

   Side Stability Hold (pg 143) 3 sets of 25 sec.
   holds

   Med-Ball Figure 8 Drill (pg 141) 3 sets of 8
   reps on each leg

5. **Flexibility Training**

   Stretches 1–13 (Chapter 17) 1 rep of 5
   inhalations/exhalations each

Week 6

MONDAY: UPPER BODY

1. **Upper Body Warm-up 15 min.**
   All 6 Crawls (pgs 59–62) 2 sets of 10 yards each
   All 8 Med-Ball Drills (pgs 63–67) 1 set of 15 throws (10 to each side when appropriate)

2. **Upper-Body Training**
   Neck
   Forward Ball Lean (pg 73) 3 sets of 20 sec.
   Side Ball Lean (pg 74) 3 sets of 20 sec. on each side
   Band Neck Training (pg 75) 3 sets of 5 reps
   Chest
   Weighted Dip (pg 93) 3 sets of 8 reps
   Floor Press (pg 95) 3 sets of 6 reps
   Back
   Wide-Grip Behind-the-Neck Pull-up (pg 124) 4 sets of 8 reps
   Arm and Hand
   Fat-Bar Hold (pg 110) 3 sets of 1 min.

3. **Core Training**
   Olympic-Bar Bus Driver (pg 148) 2 sets of 8 reps on each side
   Cable and Physioball Side Twist (pg 150) 2 sets of 8 reps on each side
   Cable and Physioball Downward Twist (pg 150) 2 sets of 8 reps on each side
   Cable and Physioball Upward Twist (pg 151) 2 sets of 6 reps on each side

4. **Flexibility Training**
   Stretches 14–23 (Chapter 17) 1 rep of 5 inhalations/exhalations each

TUESDAY: HURRICANE

1. **Warm-up 25 min.**
   All Stationary Warm-up Drills (pg 43–48) 3 sets of 10 reps
   All Movement Warm-up Drills (pg 48–50) 2 sets of 20 yards
   All Muscle Activation Exercises (pgs 51–58) 1 set of 8 reps (on each side if necessary)

2. **Heart and Lung: Hammer Session**
   Overhead Hammer Strike (pg 171) 3 sets of 8 reps on each side
   Side Hammer Strike (pg 172) 2 sets of 8 reps on each side
   Diagonal Hammer Strike (pg 172) 2 sets of 8 reps on each side

3. **Hurricane Category 4**
   Treadmill at 9, 9.5, and 10 mph and 10% grade for 25 sec. for 3 sets with Close-Grip Bench Press (pg 92) 8 reps and Chin-up (pg 121) 8 reps after each sprint.
   Treadmill at 10.5, 11, and 11.5 mph and 10% grade for 25 sec. for 3 sets with Weighted Dip (pg 93) 10 reps and Band Curl (pg 110) 10 reps after each sprint.
   Treadmill at 12, 13, and 14 mph and 10% grade for 20 sec. for 3 sets with Tire Flip (pg 107) 10 flips after each sprint.

4. **Flexibility Training**
   Stretches 1–13 (Chapter 17) 1 rep of 5 inhalations/exhalations each

THURSDAY: HURRICANE

1. **Warm-up 25 min.**
   All Stationary Warm-up Drills (pgs 43–48)
   3 sets of 10 reps
   All Movement Warm-up Drills (pg 48–50)
   2 sets of 20 yards
   All Muscle Activation Exercises (pgs 51–58)
   1 set of 8 reps (on each side if necessary)

2. **Heart and Lung: Bar Complex Session**
   2 Total Bar Complexes (pgs 184–190) of the 12
   exercises for 6 reps each, finishing each
   complex in under 1 min. 15 sec.

3. **Hurricane Category 3**
   Treadmill at 10 mph and 10% grade for 25 sec.
   for 3 sets with Reverse Cable Fly (pg 130) 10
   reps and Gi Row (pg 111) 10 reps after each
   sprint.
   Treadmill at 11 mph and 10% grade for 20 sec.
   for 3 sets with Knee-on-Chest Bent-Over
   Row (pg 80) 8 reps on each arm after each
   sprint.
   Treadmill at 12 mph and 10% grade for 20 sec.
   for 3 sets with Incline Dumbbell Clean (pg
   76) 10 reps after each sprint.

4. **Flexibility Training**
   Stretches 1–13 (Chapter 17) 1 rep of 5
   inhalations/exhalations each

FRIDAY: LOWER BODY

1. **Warm-up 10 min.**
   All Stationary Warm-up Drills (pgs 43–48)
   3 sets of 10 reps

2. **Heart and Lung: Plyo Box Jumps**
   High-Box Forward Jump (pg 178) 5 reps for
   2 sets
   Single-Leg High-Box Forward Jump (pg 178)
   5 reps on each leg for 2 sets
   Twisting High-Box Jump (pg 179) 5 reps on
   each side

3. **Lower-Body Training**
   Hips
   Cable Knee Lift (pg 197) 2 sets of 8 reps on
   each leg
   Band Guard Pull (pg 197) 2 sets of 10 reps
   Wobble Walk (ankle band) (pg 200) 2 sets of 30
   yards
   Glutes and Quads
   Step-up (pg 211) 4 sets of 5 reps on each leg
   Hamstrings
   Single-Leg Hamstring Curl (pg 221) 3 sets of 5
   reps on each leg
   Feet
   Toe-out Calf Raise (pg 227) 3 sets of 10 reps

4. **Core Training**
   Single-Leg Prone Abdominal Plank (pg 144)
   3 sets of 15 sec. holds on each leg
   Side Stability Hold (pg 143) 3 sets of 25 sec.
   holds
   Med-Ball Figure 8 Drill (pg 141) 3 sets of
   8 reps on each leg

5. **Flexibility Training**
   Stretches 1–13 (Chapter 17) 1 rep of 5
   inhalations/exhalations each

Week 7

MONDAY: UPPER BODY

1. **Upper Body Warm-up 15 min.**
   All 6 Crawls (pgs 59–62) 2 sets of 10 yards each
   All 8 Med-Ball Drills (pgs 63–67) 1 set of 15 throws (10 to each side when appropriate)

2. **Upper-Body Training**
   Neck
   Forward Ball Lean (pg 73) 3 sets of 20 sec.
   Side Ball Lean (pg 74) 3 sets of 20 sec. on each side
   Knee-on-Chest Bent-Over Row (pg 75) 3 sets of 8 reps
   Chest
   Weighted Dip (pg 93) 3 sets of 8 reps
   Floor Press (pg 95) 3 sets of 6 reps
   Back
   Wide-Grip Chin-to-Hand Pull-up (pg 124) 4 sets of 6 reps on each side
   Arm and Hand
   Band Curl (pg 110) 3 sets of 8 reps

3. **Core Training**
   Cable and Physioball Side Twist (pg 150) 2 sets of 8 reps on each side
   Cable and Physioball Downward Twist (pg 150) 2 sets of 8 reps on each side
   Cable and Physioball Upward Twist (pg 151) 2 sets of 6 reps on each side
   Cable and Physioball Suplex (pg 151) 2 sets of 6 reps on each side

4. **Flexibility Training**
   Stretches 14–23 (Chapter 17) 1 rep of 5 inhalations/exhalations each

TUESDAY: HURRICANE

1. **Warm-up 25 min.**
   All Stationary Warm-up Drills (pg 43–48) 3 sets of 10 reps
   All Movement Warm-up Drills (pg 48–50) 2 sets of 20 yards
   All Muscle Activation Exercises (pgs 51–58) 1 set of 8 reps (on each side if necessary)

2. **Heart and Lung: Ladder Session**
   All 8 Ladder Exercises (pgs 174–177) in succession for 2 times each through the ladder continuously. Rest after the first set for 2 min. and repeat 2 more sets.

3. **Hurricane Category 4**
   Treadmill at 9, 9.5, and 10 mph and 10% grade for 25 sec. for 3 sets with Power Curl (pg 213) 8 reps and Overhead Press (pg 100) 8 reps after each sprint.
   Treadmill at 10.5, 11, and 11.5 mph and 10% grade for 25 sec. for 3 sets with Power High Pull (pg 214) 8 reps after each sprint.
   Treadmill at 12, 13, and 14 mph and 10% grade for 20 sec. for 3 sets with Rolling Thunder Dead-Lift (pg 128) 6 reps on each arm after each sprint.

4. **Flexibility Training**
   Stretches 1–13 (Chapter 17) 1 rep of 5 inhalations/exhalations each

THURSDAY: HURRICANE

1. **Warm-up 25 min.**

   All Stationary Warm-up Drills (pgs 43–48)
   3 sets of 10 reps

   All Movement Warm-up Drills (pg 48–50)
   2 sets of 20 yards

   All Muscle Activation Exercises (pgs 51–58)
   1 set of 8 reps (on each side if necessary)

2. **Heart and Lung: Bar Complex Session**

   2 Total Bar Complexes (pgs 184–190) of the 12
   exercises for 6 reps each, finishing each
   complex in under 1 min. 10 sec.

3. **Hurricane Category 4**

   Treadmill at 9, 9.5, and 10 mph and 10% grade
   for 25 sec. for 3 sets with Close-Grip Bench
   Press (pg 92) 8 reps and Chin-up (pg 121) 8
   reps after each sprint.

   Treadmill at 10.5, 11, and 11.5 mph and 10%
   grade for 25 sec. for 3 sets with Weighted Dip
   (pg 93) 10 reps and Band Curl (pg 110) 10
   reps after each sprint.

   Treadmill at 12, 13, and 14 mph and 10%
   grade for 20 sec. for 3 sets with Tire Flip (pg
   107) 10 flips after each sprint.

4. **Flexibility Training**

   Stretches 1–13 (Chapter 17) 1 rep of 5
   inhalations/exhalations each

FRIDAY: LOWER BODY

1. **Warm-up 10 min.**

   All Stationary Warm-up Drills (pgs 43–48)
   3 sets of 10 reps

2. **Heart and Lung: Plyo Box Jumps**

   High-Box Forward Jump (pg 178) 5 reps for
   2 sets

   Single-Leg High-Box Forward Jump (pg 178)
   5 reps on each leg for 2 sets

   Twisting High-Box Jump (pg 179) 5 reps on
   each side

3. **Lower-Body Training**

   Hips

   Cable Knee Lift (pg 197) 2 sets of 8 reps on
   each leg

   Band Guard Pull (pg 197) 2 sets of 10 reps

   Wobble Walk (ankle band) (pg 200) 2 sets of 30
   yards

   Glutes and Quads

   Step-up (pg 211) 4 sets of 5 reps on each leg

   Weighted Lunge Walk (pg 211) 2 sets of 10 steps

   Hamstrings

   Single-Leg Hamstring Curl (pg 221) 3 sets of 5
   reps on each leg

   Feet

   Toe-in Calf Raise (pg 227) 3 sets of 10 reps

4. **Core Training**

   Single-Leg Prone Abdominal Plank (pg 144) 3
   sets of 15 sec. holds on each leg

   Abducted Side Stability Hold (pg 143) 3 sets of
   20 sec. holds

   Med-Ball Figure 8 Drill (pg 141) 3 sets of 8
   reps on each leg

5. **Flexibility Training**

   Stretches 1–13 (Chapter 17) 1 rep of 5
   inhalations/exhalations each

Week 8

MONDAY: UPPER BODY

1. **Upper Body Warm-up 15 min.**
   All 6 Crawls (pgs 59–62) 2 sets of 10 yards each
   All 8 Med-Ball Drills (pgs 63–67) 1 set of 15 throws (10 to each side when appropriate)

2. **Upper-Body Training**
   Neck
   Forward Ball Lean (pg 73) 3 sets of 20 sec.
   Side Ball Lean (pg 74) 3 sets of 20 sec. on each side
   Knee-on-Chest Bent-Over Row (pg 75) 3 sets of 8 reps
   Chest
   Weighted Dip (pg 93) 3 sets of 8 reps
   Floor Press (pg 95) 3 sets of 6 reps
   Back
   Renzo Gracie Pull-up (pg 125) 4 sets of 8 reps
   Arm and Hand
   Band Curl (pg 110) 3 sets of 10 reps

3. **Core Training**
   Cable and Physioball Side Twist (pg 150) 2 sets of 8 reps on each side
   Cable and Physioball Downward Twist (pg 150) 2 sets of 8 reps on each side
   Cable and Physioball Upward Twist (pg 151) 2 sets of 6 reps on each side
   Cable and Physioball Suplex (pg 151) 2 sets of 6 reps on each side

4. **Flexibility Training**
   Stretches 14–23 (Chapter 17) 1 rep of 5 inhalations/exhalations each

TUESDAY: HURRICANE

1. **Warm-up 25 min.**
   All Stationary Warm-up Drills (pg 43–48) 3 sets of 10 reps
   All Movement Warm-up Drills (pg 48–50) 2 sets of 20 yards
   All Muscle Activation Exercises (pgs 51–58) 1 set of 8 reps (on each side if necessary)

2. **Heart and Lung: Hammer Session**
   Overhead Hammer Strike (pg 171) 3 sets of 8 reps on each side
   Side Hammer Strike (pg 172) 2 sets of 8 reps on each side
   Diagonal Hammer Strike (pg 172) 2 sets of 8 reps on each side
   Kneeling Overhead Hammer Strike (pg 173) 2 sets of 6 reps on each side

3. **Hurricane Category 5**
   Treadmill at 9, 9.5, and 10 mph and 10% grade for 30 sec. for 3 sets with Arm-over-Arm Rope Pull (pg 108) 40 yards and Farmer's Walk (pg 106) 40 yards after each sprint.
   Treadmill at 10.5, 11, and 11.5 mph and 10% grade for 25 sec. for 3 sets with Tire Flip (pg 107) 10 flips after each sprint.
   Treadmill at 12, 13, and 14 mph and 10% grade for 20 sec. for 3 sets with Sandbag Pick-up (pg 109) 10 pick ups after each sprint.

4. **Flexibility Training**
   Stretches 1–13 (Chapter 17) 1 rep of 5 inhalations/exhalations each

THURSDAY: HURRICANE

1. **Warm-up 25 min.**
   All Stationary Warm-up Drills (pgs 43–48)
     3 sets of 10 reps
   All Movement Warm-up Drills (pg 48–50)
     2 sets of 20 yards
   All Muscle Activation Exercises (pgs 51–58)
     1 set of 8 reps (on each side if necessary)

2. **Heart and Lung: Bar Complex Session**
   3 Total Bar Complexes (pgs 184–190) of the 12
     exercises for 6 reps each, finishing each
     complex in under 1 min. 10 sec.

3. **Hurricane Category 4**
   Treadmill at 9, 9.5, and 10 mph and 10% grade
     for 25 sec. for 3 sets with Power Curl (pg
     213) 8 reps and Overhead Press (pg 100)
     8 reps after each sprint.
   Treadmill at 10.5, 11, and 11.5 mph and 10%
     grade for 25 sec. for 3 sets with Power High
     Pull (pg 214) 8 reps after each sprint.
   Treadmill at 12, 13, and 14 mph and 10%
     grade for 20 sec. for 3 sets with Rolling
     Thunder Dead-Lift (pg 128) 6 reps on each
     arm after each sprint.

4. **Flexibility Training**
   Stretches 1–13 (Chapter 17) 1 rep of 5
     inhalations/exhalations each

FRIDAY: LOWER BODY

1. **Warm-up 10 min.**
   All Stationary Warm-up Drills (pgs 43–48)
     3 sets of 10 reps

2. **Heart and Lung: Plyo Box Jumps**
   High-Box Forward Jump (pg 178) 5 reps for
     2 sets
   Single-Leg High-Box Forward Jump (pg 178)
     2 sets of 5 reps on each leg
   Twisting High-Box Jump (pg 179) 5 reps on
     each side

3. **Lower-Body Training**
   Hips
   Cable Knee Lift (pg 197) 2 sets of 8 reps on
     each leg
   Band Guard Pull (pg 197) 2 sets of 10 reps
   Wobble Walk (ankle band) (pg 200) 2 sets of 30
     yards
   Glutes and Quads
   Step-up (pg 211) 4 sets of 5 reps on each leg
   Weighted Lunge Walk (pg 211) 2 sets of 10
     steps
   Hamstrings
   Single-Leg Hamstring Curl (pg 221) 3 sets of
     5 reps on each leg
   Feet
   Toe-in Calf Raises (pg 227) 3 sets of 10 reps

4. **Core Training**
   Single-Leg Prone Abdominal Plank (pg 144)
     3 sets of 15 sec. holds on each leg
   Abducted Side Stability Hold (pg 143) 3 sets of
     20 sec. holds
   Med-Ball Figure 8 Drill (pg 141) 3 sets of 8
     reps on each leg

5. **Flexibility Training**
   Stretches 1–13 (Chapter 17) 1 rep of 5
     inhalations/exhalations each

ABOUT THE AUTHOR

MARTIN ROONEY MHS, PT, CSCS, NASM

Martin Rooney is one of the most sought-after fitness professionals in the world. He has Master of Health Science and Bachelor of Physical Therapy degrees from the Medical University of South Carolina. He also holds a Bachelor of Arts in Exercise Science from Furman University.

Martin was a member of the United States Bobsled Team from 1995–1997 and in 2000, and a four-time All Conference MVP performer in Track and Field at Furman. Martin is currently a purple belt in Brazilian Jiu Jitsu under Ricardo Almeida and a black belt in Kodokan Judo under Sensei Matsumura and Olympian Teimoc Johnston-Ono of the prestigious New York Athletic Club.

Martin has been the martial arts consultant for the New York Giants and New York Jets and is a fitness columnist on the editorial counsel for Brazil's *Gracie Magazine*. He has also traveled as far as Brazil, Japan, and the Middle East to conduct seminars and help prepare world-class fighters for competitions such as PRIDE, the UFC, and the Abu Dhabi World Submission Grappling Championships. In addition to training many world-champion martial artists, Martin has also been a speed and conditioning consultant to the New York Giants, Cincinnati Bengals, Arizona State University, Oregon State University, the University of Alabama, Montana State University, as well as other athletes from the NFL, MLB, NBA, WNBA, and numerous top Division I colleges across the country. He has also trained numerous Olympians, including one gold and four silver medalists. Martin also developed one of the top NFL Combine training programs in the country, producing the fastest athlete at the 2001, 2004, 2005, and 2006 NFL Combine and first-place finishers at ten different positions, including five all-time records.

Martin has lectured for Perform Better, the American College of Sports Medicine, the College Strength and Conditioning Coaches Association, and the National Strength and Conditioning Association, and has been commissioned by Nike to run speed-testing camps at a number of major universities. Martin has been featured on ESPN, Sports New York, Fox Sports Net, the NFL Network, and NBC.com and in the *New York Times, The Sporting News, Stack* magazine, *Sports Illustrated for Kids,* and *Outside* magazine. He has written another training text, called "Train to Win," and has produced a ten-part DVD series on the Parisi Training Method.

Currently, Martin is COO and director of training of the Parisi Speed School. The Parisi Speed School is launching its national franchise opportunity under Martin's leadership, and there are already over thirty franchises in twenty states across the country sold in addition to five company-owned stores in New Jersey.

Martin lives in Fair Lawn, New Jersey, with his wife, Amanda, and their two children, Sofia and Kristina.

To find out about upcoming seminars or to host a Martin Rooney seminar, go to www.trainingforwarriors.com.

ACKNOWLEDGMENTS

Although it could be argued that this book is an eventual product of all the people I have met in my life, here is the short list of people that without whom this book would surely never have happened: Renzo Gracie, Ricardo Almeida, Bill Parisi, John Derent, Luca Atalla, Joe Sampieri.

Without any warriors to train, I would never have had anything to write about. The following is a list of the warriors that have helped shape me and subsequently, the *Training for Warriors* system.

Roger Gracie, Rolles Gracie, Ryan Gracie, Igor Gracie, Gregor Gracie, Kyra Gracie, Daniel Gracie, Rodrigo Gracie, Gene Dunn, Raphael "Gordihno" Correa, Flavio Almeida, Alan Teo, Sean Alvarez, Teimoc Johnston-Ono, Neil Wolfson, Jamal Patterson, Fabio Leopoldo, Marcio Feitosa, Alexandre "Soca" Carneiro, Braulio Estima, Shintaro Higashi, Jimmy Vennetti, Dr. Arthur Canario, Dr. Anthony Caterisano, Dr. Steven Stoller, Alvaro Romano, Ajay James, Celita Schutz, Carl Masaro, Romulo Barral, Renato Migliaccio, Kazuo Misaki, Joel Brutus, Delson Heleno, Joe "Big House" Kenn, Dr. Jose Alfredo Padilha, Dante Rivera, Tom DeBlass, Todd Hays, Mark Colangelo, Jamie Cruz, Pete Lawson, Barry Friedberg, Matt Krieger, Jamie Crowder, Jonas Sahratian, Marcelo Aller, Aziz Bendriss, Nik Fekete, Richard Mendoza, Jim Gorman, Owen Tunney, Bill Scarola, Rich Thurston, Adam Singer, Dave Maver, John Rallo, Harrison Bernstein, and Sheik Tahnoon Bin Zayed Al Nayan.

I would like to thank the Renzo Gracie Academy and the NYAC Judo club. Both places have offered me an education that no university could ever dream to provide.

I would like to thank the IFL for their support of the book and Lucas Noonan, who without his hard work, there would be no exercise photos to follow.

I would like to thank Heather Campanile, R.D., for all her help with the nutrition section and on the sample meal plans.

I would like to thank *Gracie Magazine*. Without its deadlines, I would never have been forced to learn as much about this subject as I have over the last decade.

Thanks to my editors, Stephanie Meyers and Matthew Benjamin (and all the people at HarperCollins who believed in this book), for dealing with me and my type A+ personality through the arduous process of making this project come to life.

Finally, I would like to thank my family. Most importantly this includes my wife, Amanda, and daughters, Sofia and Kristina, who have all been patient with me during my late-night writing/editing and with my missed weekends traveling to events to gain experience. I would also like to thank my parents for always allowing me to dare greatly.

PHOTO CREDITS